Rhythm of the Veda: Know your Devas

Sushrut Badhe

DEDICATION

To the transformers of the future

The Clarion Call pierced through the first dark cloud
Every mortal ear heard the sound, clear and loud.
Ecstatic skies thundered flaunting the silver lining
Ushering moist blind eyes- " The Heroes are coming".

CONTENTS

FOREWORD	5
PREFACE	9
PROLOGUE	14
1 The hymns, the Rishis & The Devas	15
2 Introducing the Devas	20
3 Agni and the legend of the Angiras	27
4 The cow, the bull & the luminous herds	33
5 Usha – the dawn divine	40
6 The truth of Varuna	46
7 Indra – the lord of the illumined mind	52
8 Soura Suktam – A hymn to Surya	56
9 The flow of Vayu	62
10. Vishnu – the friend of man	68
11. Saraswati – the river and the Goddess	72
12. The hymn to man- the last Sukta	76
EPILOGUE	80
The aim of Midam symbolised	81
Krishna's Butter Project & Midam Charitable Trust Publications	82

ACKNOWLEDGEMENT

To Sri M.R.Damle, my master who made a वेडा *(Veda-fool)*

write a book on वेदा *(Veda - knowledge)*

I also remain indebted to Mary Premilaji for editing this book.

FOREWORD

Lokmanya Bal Gangadhar Tilak (1856 – 1920) who published *The Arctic Home in the Vedas* in 1903 endorsed the theory of first president of Boston University William Fairfield Warren (1833 –1929) that early man lived in the North Pole, which was a land mass in the post glacial era. In the early geological ages, the Alps were low, the Himalayas not yet upheaved, Asia and Africa were represented only by a group of islands and an equable and uniform climate prevailed over the whole surface of the globe. Warren noted how, in those days, Homer, the legendary author of the Iliad and the Odyssey, considered as the central works of ancient Greek literature, and the ancient Roman poet Virgil and later the Greek poet Hesiod, active between 750 and 650 BCE, all placed Atlas or his world pillar at the "ends of the earth", meaning the far northern arctic regions, while Euripides related Atlas to the Pole Star. Italian poet Dante Alighieri (1265-1321) in *The Divine Comedy* emerges out of the dark nether world of hell to the South Pole and then to the shore of Mount Purgatory, in the uninhabited southern hemisphere, as opposed to the North Pole representing Paradise.

Based on Warren's book *Cradle of the Human Race at the North Pol*e, published in 1885, that placed the destruction of the original Arctic home at the last Ice Age and the commencement of the post-Glacial period at 10,000 to 8000 BCE, Lokmanya Tilak, a great astronomer, timed the Vedas to the Orion constellation - 5000 to 3000 BCE - when the vernal equinox was in Orion. "Lokmanya writes, "At the North Pole, one sees the heavenly dome above seems to revolve around one like a potter's wheel. The stars will not rise and set but move round and round in horizontal planes during the long night of six months. The Sun, when it is above the horizon for six months, would also appear to revolve in the same way." Rig-Vedic hymns can be traced to the early part of this period. The destruction of the original Arctic home had taken place by the last Ice Age followed by the commencement of the post-Glacial period. The survivors of the human race roamed over the northern parts of Europe and Asia in search of land suitable for new settlements. The "bards of the race, based on the memories of the Arctic home passed on by their ancestors, sang and recorded those memories in the form of Brahmana and Aranyaka texts with heavy doses of their own imagination and reason.

Canadian philosopher Ian MacDougall Hacking (b. 1936) says, "Memory is a powerful tool in quests for understanding, justice, and knowledge. It raises consciousness. It heals some wounds, restores dignity, and prompts uprisings." Vedas are primarily the memory of our ancestors of what they felt in observing the natural spectacle at the Arctic Circle. They coded it for posterity to helping them to stay anchored to the infinite intelligence. And like any other code, it has to be inserted into a larger body and operated upon. This book of Sushrut Badhe is about this booting of the primal mental energy CPU, what Carl Jung (1875 –1961) called "Collective Unconscious" and the purpose of life as "integrating the conscious and the unconscious". Maharishi Arvind (1872 – 1950) explained it as "The Life Divine" saying that "True knowledge is not attained by thinking, it ought to be accessed from within, It is what you are; it is what you become."

It is important to differentiate between what Maharishi Arvind called "The spiritual life, the religious life and the ordinary human life." What most of us are doing, most of time, is living our ordinary lives out as feast for our senses. This is not only a cut-off from our own true self, which is the Divine, but is also bereft of reason and insensitive to the conscience. Like Zombies, we are moved around by the habits of our minds, our bodily impulses for pleasure and fears. This lifestyle makes one drained of vitality, and the gift of life is indeed withered away. Goswami Tulsidas called it the supreme stupidity of throwing away the Parasmani for a shining crystal glass ((Ramcharitmanans, Uttar Kanda, Doha 44, Chaupai 2,3 and 4):

नर तनु पाइ बिषयँ मन देहीं। पलटि सुधा ते सठ बिष लेहीं॥
ताहि कबहुँ भल कहइ न कोई। गुंजा ग्रहइ परस मनि खोई॥
आकर चारि लच्छ चौरासी। जोनि भ्रमत यह जिव अबिनासी॥

Wasting human life in sensory pleasures
Act of foolishness of highest order, turning nectar into poison
Exchanging enlightenment for intoxication.
What good is that mind – exchanging a shining shell
For a philosopher's stone – suffering torments of millions of lives
Immortal soul goes deluded.

The religious life is another Zombie way of living, with the difference that instead of our senses and instinct, the tenets and rules of some sect or creed are guiding us. It is a less dangerous situation but hardly beneficial. The religious life may be the first approach to the spiritual, but it is just that. When Dante Alighieri in *The Divine Comedy* approaches the gate of Hell, he sees hordes of people crowding the gate, not allowed inside. When he asks his companion Virgil, who these people are, Virgil tells, they are opportunists. As they are ordinary wrongdoers but not sinners, they are not allowed entry into Hell. The religious people are like those crowded at the gate; they have not yet accessed the Divinity and are indeed caught up in rituals.

The spiritual life is all about a change of consciousness so that consciousness can find the true being and move towards that so that it can establish living contact and eventually union with the Divine. Maharishi Arvind says, "For the spiritual seeker this change of consciousness is the one thing he seeks and nothing else matters." Basically a gifted poet, Sushrut has captured the harmony of these codes and felt their power of resonating the Cosmic Frequency in the process. I loved every word of this book and could feel the Divine so alive, captured from the Vedas and transmitted to the reader, who may have the fortune of receiving it.

Arun Tiwari

Hyderabad

November 2019

Prof. Arun Kumar Tiwari is an Indian missile scientist, author, and professor. He has written several books and co-authored 5 books with Dr. APJ Abdul Kalam, including Wings of Fire, the autobiography of Dr. APJ Abdul Kalam, former President of India and was also a member of the advisory team of the President. Published in 1999, Wings of Fire has become a modern classic with over 30 reprints selling over a million copies and was translated into 18 languages.

INTRODUCTION

Vedas are the earliest texts of ancient Indian knowledge tradition. The Sanskrit words of Vedic hymns are etymological in nature and therefore, the meaning of Vedic words may change according to the context. Traditionally, the meaning of Vedic Sanskrit words can be described in three different ways, i.e., Adhibhautik (natural), Adhidaivik (supernatural) and Adhyatmik (spiritual). Sayanacharya wrote a commentary on Vedas following the Adhibhautik etymology whereas Yaska's Nirukta provides the Adhidaivik interpretation of Vedic hymns. The tradition of Upanishads propounded the Adhyatmik meaning of mantras. Following the Upanishadic tradition, Sri Aurobindo has written the Adhyatmik commentary of Vedic hymns.

It has been quite challenging for scholars to understand and comprehend the Adhyatmik translation of Vedic hymns. Sh. Sushrut Badhe, a young author and Manasa-putra of Sri Aurobindo tradition has attempted to unravel the mysteries and presented the basics of Adhyatmik translation of Vedic hymns in his book titled "Rhythm of the Veda: Know Your Devas". This book shows a true path to know the Vedic Devatas in the Adhyatmik etymology. I have no words to compliment the young author for his scholarly work and dedication. I recommend this book for all inquisitive readers who aim to explore the true essence of Vedas.

Vedveer Arya

Delhi
January 2020

Vedveer Arya is presently Finance Manager (Maritime and Systems) at Ministry of Defence, New Delhi. A former Director (Finance) for the Agni, Area Defence missile programmes and other tactical missile programmes in the DRDO, Ministry of Defence, he is also an author and

Sushrut Badhe

Sanskrit scholar specialising in Paninian grammar, including the Mahabhashya of Patanjali and was awarded the Radhakrishnan and CD Deshmukh memorial Gold medals in the process. He and has authored -The Chronology of India: From Mahabharata to Medieval Era - Vol I & II, among other books which shed light on the chronological errors in the history based on the contemporary archaeological and scriptural evidence

PREFACE

Normally, it would be considered illogical and foolhardy for a mechanical engineer with no formal education in either Sanskrit or literature to dare to attempt a commentary on the oldest scripture known to mankind. But then again, nothing has happened in my life from 2010 onwards, ever since I met my teacher, Sri M.R.Damleji, has conformed to the definition of normal logic. My first introduction to the Veda came when I heard him chant an Agni Sukta during a yagnya and I was most intrigued by the rhythm of his chanting and overwhelmed when he explained to me the meaning of the sukta in the light of Sri Aurobindo. And on that day, I learnt that I, like most Indians, was genetically linked to the mystic seers or Rishis of the Vedas by virtue of one of the many 'Gotras' that identified the bloodline of the founding Rishi. To learn that the blood of the Vedic Rishis flowed through my veins suddenly made the Rishis seem a little less distant. But this was not the reason why I chose to try to write a commentary about knowing the Devas of the Rig Veda.

In 2012, I had an opportunity to engage in a collaborative study of the therapeutic effect of Vedic Chanting on the behaviour of children with autism where my main task involved sitting along with the children and listening to vedic hymns chanted by Damleji thrice a day for a period of more than four months. The study went on to receive "The Best Poster" in an international scientific conference –ISHG, Ahmedabad in 2014 and my parents noticed distinct behavioural changes in me . But this too was not the reason why I chose to try to write a commentary to know the Devas of the Rig Veda.

In 2013, Damleji was kind enough to allow me to accompany him on a spiritual journey to different sacred places in Maharashtra. Among the places visited, the sacred tree or Ajaana Vriksha at Alandi, that grew over the Sanjeevan Samadhi of the great realized one Sant. Dnyaneshwar, also revered as Mauli or Mother all across Maharashtra, deserves a special mention. Mauli, despite being an enlightened soul, was ostracized by the society throughout his childhood and mocked by the orthodox Vedic scholars and elders initially but later on was acknowledged by the entire village when they witnessed his many miracles. The story of how he made the Vedic hymns emerge out of the mouth of a buffalo before an assembly of the learned fascinated me the most and I was excited to visit the Ajaana Vriksha tree. I had just learnt that eating even one leaf that falls from the sacred tree improves one's intelligence. Recognizing my scarcity, I ate four leaves and prayed to Mauli for a miracle. A couple of years later I succeeded in writing a version of the Bhagavad Gita and in the subsequent year also the Isha, Kena, Manudkya and Sri Aurobindo's Upanishad in rhyme. These were declared records by India Book of Records, Limca book of records and other record verifying organizations. But neither was this the reason why I chose to try to write a commentary on knowng the Devas of the Rig Veda.

To be honest, the real reason remains unknown to me. I haven't interacted with the Devas like the Angiras sages did in their hymns or seen their celestial carriages traversing the skies like the Atris and other Rishis. I am like a blind man looking up to the sun. I cannot see the Rig Vedic sun but can certainly feel the warmth of its rays falling upon me and also point to its direction. I haven't been capable of seeing the brilliance of the Devas with my eyes, but I certainly have perceived their warmth through the hymns of the Rishis and hence can say with certainty that the forgotten Vedic deities of India are not asleep. They are very much in action all around us as they have always been.

It is this experience that I have sought to share with my readers through this small book. This book is a compilation and modification of articles from the Spirit of the Vedas series that is being featured in the monthly journal –*Sri Aurobindo's Action* whose aim is to help bring about the resurgence of India.

Eleven prominent yet lesser known Vedic Dieties of the Rig Veda have been selected and their hymns have been versified in rhyme with a brief commentary on the symbolism and inner meanings. The rhyme rendition and description has been done solely in the light of Sri Aurobindo's 'Secret of the Veda' and simple illustrations have been provided for picturing the functions of as many Gods as possible. A short bio of the composing Rishi has also been given at the end of each hymn. The aim is to provide the present generation of readers with a key to connect with the Vedic Network of the Rishis and the Devas. If you like the book, share it with friends and pass on the word and if you don't please do take your time to send your criticism.

Regards and Prayers

Sushrut Badhe

PROLOGUE

For Nine days, the inferno at Nalanda burnt
Hoping to erase all the sacred texts that were learnt
Other sanctums of learning too were then raided
Knowledge suffered distortions and struggled unaided

Over generations this loss compounded and spread
The hidden wisdom was lost- unheard and never read
The devilish ploy was that the light be forever buried
And down the ages nothing was passed or carried

But little was really known or understood by man
That all of this too was part of the grand plan
Several sacred texts were destroyed in time's course
But no force on earth could touch the divine source

From the same planes where the truth was heard
Would reverberate once more the first word
Newer Vedas too would once more come-
From this churning the world too shall immortal become

Across the oceans shall burst the volcanoes of light
Flooding and cleansing the plagued lands of blight
The Sons of Angiras, Atri and the other Rishis shall rise
And one hotar shall perform Vishwajit Yagnya- the final sacrifice!

1 THE HYMNS, THE RISHIS & THE DEVAS

"Is there at all or is there still a secret of the Veda?"

With this profound opening question, Sri Aurobindo began his treatise on the primordial text whose very name means knowledge, '*The Secret of the Veda*'. A century has passed since his first translations and writings on the Veda appeared in '*Arya*' and yet we have for some uncognizable reason distanced ourselves from the Vedas- the seed scriptures that have shaped the developments of science, philosophy and art over the ages. A hundred thousand temples, and this figure is by no means an exaggeration, have sprung up across the length and breadth of our temple land but neither their sanctums nor their walls have offered space to the Vedic deities who were antecedents to all the Gods deified in the sacred structures.

While the text of the sole surviving retention of the complete Rig Veda, whose authenticity has been verified and accepted, is very much with us, the ancient Vedic Sanskrit used in it has ceased to dance on the tip of the tongues of even the most learned amongst modern Sanskrit scholars further distancing the already alienated masses away from the real meaning of this powerful spiritual treasure. European scholars and philosophers, with and without questionable motives, have worked laboriously in fixing and assigning meanings to the hymns contained in the scripture and have not been very successful in their attempt as is evident from the gross inconsistencies arising out of their purportedly rational interpretation as clearly highlighted by Sri Aurobindo in his treatise. The multi-roots of the Sanskrit words have been used far too liberally to create a narrative suggesting that the hymns and Vedas are but ritualistic invocations of barbarians to different Nature-elements deified as fierce and all-powerful Gods. The interpretation that the sages sought to invoke the Elements only to grant protection from enemies, wealth and food for their respective clans can be declared to be as far as possible from the truth. While reducing the motive of the sages and composers of these hymns to a desire for food and wealth is absolute sacrilege, the entire blame of this monumental blunder cannot be passed on to foreign shoulders.

"The modern theory of the Veda starts with the conception for which Sayana is responsible, of the Vedas as the hymnal of an early, primitive and largely barbaric society crude in its moral and religious conceptions, rude in its social structure and entirely childlike in its outlook upon the world that environed it." - Sri Aurobindo, CWSA Vol 15, p. 25.

Indian scholars, on the other hand, unwittingly created an opening for the scholars of the West to foray into the impregnable and confounding philological fortress of the scriptures, stamp their interpretations upon them and validate them by retaining the interpretation of the Indian scholars as their reference. A number of factors made this intrusion possible and one can only hypothesize that the prevalent social and cultural transitions led to the purely ritualistic interpretations of the Indian scholars. A great change was taking place in ancient India in the post-Vedic Era. The sun of the age of intuition was setting and a new age of reason was beginning. Even the Sanskrit language, which was a lot more symbolic and poetic in the Vedas, began to be replaced with a Sanskrit that was more focused on philosophy and structuring. The focus shifted from interpreting the Vedas to founding the Upanishads or the Vedantas and as Sri Aurobindo points out a dichotomy of Veda and Vedanta began to manifest.

" A sharp practical division came into being, effective though never entirely recognized in theory between Veda and Vedanta, a distinction which might be expressed in the formula, Veda for the priests, the Vedanta for the sages" - Sri Aurobindo, CWSA Vol 15, p. 15.

The Upanishadic age was soon followed by the age of the Puranas which eventually led to the birth of the vernacular languages. The rise of Buddhism also furthered the side-lining of the Vedas; newer religious systems began to occupy a prominent place in the society and the Sanskrit language too began to lose prominence among the masses. Only a selected group of Pandits or scholars remained who continued to pass on the text religiously from generation to generation for they understood that the texts were sacrosanct and thus diligently guarded their sanctity and passed them on word for word and sound for sound. While their scrupulous attachment to adhering rigidly to lexicon and diction ensured that the Vedic text was preserved, their approach, which was often despotic and led to fear mongering, prevented the masses from touching the scriptures. For instance we have, in the Brahmanas, the story of a sage Twashtri who while performing his sacrifice chanted the words 'Indra' and 'Shatru' in the wrong notes with catastrophic results because the wrong pronunciation completely reversed the meaning of the chant. Instead of empowering his son to slay Indra, he caused his son to be slain by Indra, thus highlighting the drastic consequences of hymns of invocation wrongly uttered.

While we are without doubt grateful that these texts have been preserved in their original forms, in the handing over of the Vedas from the sage to the priest and from the priest to the scholar, great damage was done. The original meaning of the sages was lost and only the ritualistic interpretation of the priests remained in the scholastic rendering of the Vedas.

"For even in the earlier days of classical erudition the ritualistic view of the Veda was already dominant, the original sense of the words, the lines, the allusions, the clue to the structure of the thought had been long lost or obscured; nor was there in the erudite that intuition or that spiritual experience which might have partly recovered the lost secret. In such a field, mere learning, especially when it is accompanied by an ingenious scholastic mind, is often a snare as a guide."
– Sri Aurobindo, CWSA Vol 15, p. 19.

If we were wholly to accept the Western Indologists we would have to come to the conclusion that the Vedas are naught but a collection of hymns composed by barbarous and fair skinned Aryans who wanted their Gods in whose favour the hymns were chanted to grant them cows, horses, rich food and prosperity and drive away the dark-skinned Dravidians who were always trying to steal their cattle.

And if we are to wholly accept the likes of the scholastic Indian renditions, the hymns are naught but a collection of ceremonial rituals to various Gods which needed to be performed meticulously and without any flaws to ensure that the Gods be merciful and pleased so that they grant the priest of the sacrifice and all the others involved longevity, prosperity and plenty of food and cattle.

In both these interpretations, a very important factor is altogether ignored: the very composers of the hymns, the realised sages. The premise that the Rishi's or spiritually accomplished Vedic Sages composed the hymns to gain material possessions seems absurd and banal, making one wonder how this interpretation came into existence in the first place. This is where the multi-roots of the words of the Sanskrit language serve as the key to solving the many inconsistencies arising out of arbitrary assignment of English meanings to Sanskrit root words. In his treatise, in the chapter 'The Foundations of the Psychological Theory', Sri Aurobindo has successfully deconstructed the myth furthered by the misattribution of the fight between darkness and light mentioned in the Vedas to an Aryan-Dravidian battle, and has clearly established that the Vedic hymns are actually formulae or blueprints of realizations of the Rishis that were recorded after the attainment of personal victories on spiritual planes with the aim for providing a key for future seekers to attain the same. While a cursory glance reveals a simple outward ritualistic meaning, the cryptographic nature of the hymns becomes clear to us when we observe the symbolism embedded in the verses with a careful and trained eye.

"We have concluded that the Angiras Rishis are bringers of the Dawn, rescuers of the Sun out of the darkness, but that this Dawn, Sun, Darkness are figures used with a spiritual significance. The central conception of the Veda is the conquest of the Truth out of the darkness of Ignorance and by the conquest of the Truth the conquest also of Immortality" - Sri Aurobindo, CWSA Vol 15, p. 241.

The legends of the Angiras, Panis, Vritras and Dasyus are to be treated as parables and their symbolism is to be discerned if we are to understand the Veda in the true Spirit. It is this Spirit that I wish to connect to and so, using the key provided in 'The Secret of the Veda', I will attempt to break the seal stamped upon the Veda by the present day ritualistic interpretations. While I have no qualms about my capacity or my erudition as I am fully aware that I do not hold the necessary academic qualification to comment on these sacred scriptures, I understand that no institution can deny me the right to attempt a poetic transcreation of the hymns of the Rig Veda.

The Marathi saint Tukaram, who was chastised by the society in his earlier days for his interpretation of the Vedas and later on revered as a realized soul, in his compilation of works – 'Tukaram Gatha' lashed out very fiercely at the orthodox conformists and scholars of the ritualistic school of interpretation.

वेदाचा तो अर्थ आम्हासी च ठावा। येरांनी वाहावा भार माथा॥
खादल्याची गोडी देखिल्यासी नाही। भार धन वाही मजुरीचे॥

- Tukaram Gatha,2266

"That meaning of the Veda, Only I claim to verily understand and know
Carrying the burden of the texts on their heads, the others can go
The experience of sweetness that comes from taste, by seeing one cannot share
May the porters for their labour of carrying the goods, receive their due fare."

Quoting him, I begin my journey to connect myself and my readers with the spirit of the Rig Veda-its hymns, sages and the Devas.

2 INTRODUCING THE DEVAS

Almost every verse of the Rig Vedic scripture is in itself pregnant with a twin meaning- the exoteric and the esoteric. Our focus will be on the esoteric significance of the verses. We will not be following an exclusive exoteric approach as propounded by the followers of the purely ritualistic theory of the Veda, not only because I see no merit in pursuing the same worn out road that has been pursued over and over again over centuries with absolute rigidity, but also because we can effortlessly understand the beautiful and occult inner dimension of the Veda, simply by treading the sunlit path in the light of Sri Aurobindo's 'Psychological Theory' according to which the Rig Veda is '*a Scripture not confused in thought or primitive in its substance, not a medley of heterogeneous or barbarous elements, but one, complete and self-conscious in its purpose and in its purport, veiled indeed by the cover, sometimes thick, sometimes transparent, of another and material sense, but never losing sight even for a single moment of its high spiritual aim and tendency*' - Sri Aurobindo, CWSA Vol 15, p. 47.

The Rig Veda in total contains 1017 hymns scattered across 10 Books or Mandalas. Each Hymn is dedicated to a single deity (Agni, Varuna, Soma etc) or twin deities (Mitra-Varuna, Soma-Rudra, etc.) or multiple deities, and sometimes all the deities combined (Vishwedevas) composed by the mystic Vedic sages. While it is our purpose to delve deep into the Rig Veda and re-connect to the primal scripture, a complete study of all the 1000 plus hymns is well beyond the scope of this attempt due to obvious constraints of capacity and time. Unsure of how to begin, I approached my teacher, Damleji, to discover the best way to begin this attempt and, in response to my question, I received a cryptic answer that the best way to begin would be 'by beginning'. And so I have decided to begin with a simplistic and straight forward approach to the Veda by turning first to the Gods of the Vedas.

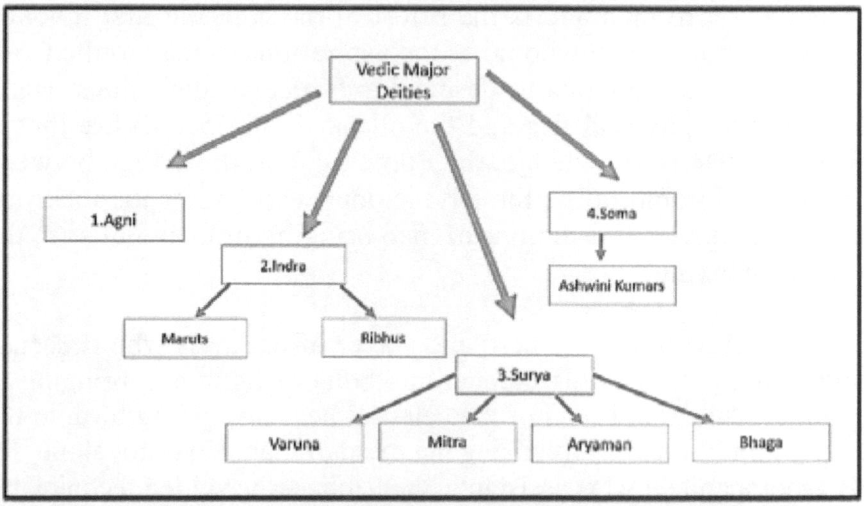

A) Schematic of Four Major Vedic Deities & Associate Powers

Sri Aurobindo recognized four major deities of prime significance, in terms of their powers and roles, among all the Rig Vedic deities. They are Agni, Indra, Surya and Soma in the order of invokation of their presence. This is the general order of invocation followed by the Vedic seers but it may not be mis-interpreted as an order of importance, for all the deities are ultimately different forces and powers of the One truth – '*tad ekam*' as Sri Aurobindo has clearly explained in his 'hymns to the Mystic Fire' and described as the kernel of the doctrine of the Veda.

" The Gods, the powers of Light and Truth are powers and names of the One, each God is himself all the Gods or carries them in him; there is the one Truth, tat satyam, and one bliss to which we must rise" - Sri Aurobindo, CWSA Vol 16. p. 21.

I have created a schematic of the primary Gods and their associate powers who enable their manifestation and operation on the material plane to aid in getting a better understanding of their names and roles. The first of the Gods is Agni – the blazing ascender, the one who is closest to man and is the priest of the call, the first invoked in the sacrifice, the one who takes the aspirations of man to the Gods and also invites the Gods to descend and receive their dues. He is both the outer physical fire and the all purifiying occult fire that is within man. He is knowledge, the Force of Will, the bridge between mortality and immortality, the Divine doer who ignites the inner aspiration and powers the actions of man bringing light and bliss to the whole of mankind.

Next is invoked Indra, the hero and slayer of darkness who descends from the heavens with his thunderours bolts of ligntning, bringing to the mortal plane the waters of the celestial heavens, giving birth to the faculty of intuition and Divinising the mind of man. He is not alone, for he is accompanied by his assistants, the Ribhus- the skilled technicians, his human powers, who aid the upward ascension of man and participate in the work of the sacrifice to shape, mould and transform the mind of man. For his actions of conquest and valor, Indra is aided by the roaring dieties-the Maruts, who function behind thought and speech and help in slaying the Vritras – the forces of darkness that veil the light of the sun of supreme truth.

The next primary diety is Surya – the Sun and Lord of Supreme truth who floods the creation with his truth illuminations, nourishing all life forms and bathing our souls in light, dispelling the unending nights of darkness by giving birth to the beautiful and luminous dawn of truth. Surya is accompanied by four other powers- the just and fierce Varuna seated on his throne in the heavens, the all loving, compassionate friend of all beings – Mitra, Aryaman- the pure one who aids every right action and inspiration and Bhaga – the force that participates in the right enjoyment and spreads the elixer of happiness.

Next is Soma- the Divine and complete bliss, the power that raises in man the immortal consciousness, the perfect and complete happiness, the ambrosial nectar of true Ananda in the vital, physical and mental. Soma is aided by the nimble twin Gods- The Ashwin Kumars, the Divine healing horseman who ride swiftly to bring in us the divine ascension.

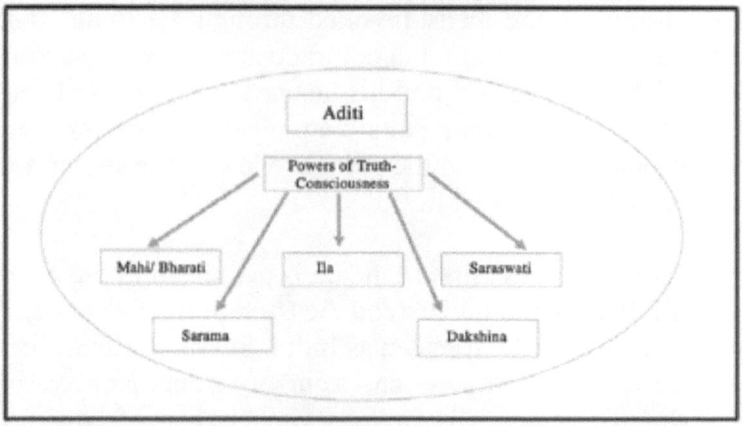

B) Schematic of Female Deities of the Rig Veda

Just as there are the major masculine powers, each of the Gods has his female energy and we come across a number of female dieties in the Rig Veda. We first come across the universal and infinite mother of all Gods – Aditi. She is the first and we have the five powers of Sat that manifest everywhere in the universe. Mahi/Bharati – the word that births the creations from the Divine source, Ila – the word that grants the vision of truth, Saraswati- The word of inspiration that furthers the new creation, Sarama – the heavenly hound that descends and penetrates the innermost dark caves of the subconscient to discover the hidden light, and Dakshina, the Divine distributor who ensures that all the Gods receive their rightful dues from the offerings of the sacrifice.

The Origins of the Divine trinity of Brahma (The Creater), Vishnu (the Preserver) and Mahesh (the Destroyer) in the Puranas too can be retraced to the the Trinity observed in the hymns to Brahmanaspati, Visnu and Rudra. We also find many dieties, such as Vayu, Dadhikravan, Parajanya, but we will be dealing with each of these as and when we come across them as we journey through the hymns.

The relations of the Rishis/ Rishikas with the Vedic Devatas is also a very fascnating aspect of the Rig Veda for each seer established a distinct relation with the Deity invoked through the hymn. The same diety becomes a father, a parent, a comrade and friend depending upon the nature of the Vedic Rishi and his/her proximity to the Diety. Each Hymn of a sage had a rhythm and style typical of the composer. When we delve into each hymn from the point of view of the singer, the experience becomes all the more blissful.

Since the first hymn of the first Mandala is dedicated to the major deity Agni, we will first seek to understand the truth of the Deva-Agni before moving on to the other deities such as Indra, Surya, Varuna, Vishnu and Vayu. We will also, in the process, cast a cursory glance at the Vedic Sages and their styles of expression, including the symbolism of the cow, the bull and the luminous herds, the Goddess of Divine Dawn- Usha and Saraswati.

A discussion on the various other Gods such as Soma, Rudra, Ashwins, Maruts, Vishwedevas, and also the consumers of light, the creatures of darkness such as Vritras and Valas, has been purposely omitted as beyond the scope of this current exploration whose sole aim is to briefly introduce the readers to the Gods of the Vedas and the spirit in which the great Vedic Rishis crafted their hymns.

With this introduction, I begin with the rhyme rendition of the Hymn that initiated the beginning of the sacred scripture: the first hymn of the Rig Veda,

अग्निमीळे पुरोहितं यज्ञस्य देवमृत्विजम् ।
होतारं रत्नधातमम् ॥ १.००१.०१
अग्निः पूर्वेभिर्ऋषिभिरीड्यो नूतनैरुत ।
स देवाँ एह वक्षति ॥ १.००१.०२
अग्निना रयिमश्नवत्पोषमेव दिवेदिवे ।
यशसं वीरवत्तमम् ॥ १.००१.०३

अग्ने यं यज्ञमध्वरं विश्वतः परिभूरसि ।
स इद्देवेषु गच्छति ॥ १.००१.०४
अग्निर्होता कविक्रतुः सत्यश्चित्रश्रवस्तमः ।
देवो देवेभिरा गमत् ॥ १.००१.०५
यदङ्ग दाशुषे त्वमग्ने भद्रं करिष्यसि ।
तवेत्तत्सत्यमङ्गिरः ॥ १.००१.०६
उप त्वाग्ने दिवेदिवे दोषावस्तर्धिया वयम् ।
नमो भरन्त एमसि ॥ १.००१.०७
राजन्तमध्वराणां गोपामृतस्य दीदिविम् ।
वर्धमानं स्वे दमे ॥ १.००१.०८
स नः पितेव सूनवेऽग्ने सूपायनो भव ।
सचस्वा नः स्वस्तये ॥ १.००१.०९

I revere *Agni*- the foremost priest, the fire sacrifice's lord,
The boon of splendour and prosperity, you do verily accord.|1|

To Agni, the sages- both ancient and present, offer their devotion
To the herald of the Gods, they pay homage with adulation.|2|

By Agni's grace, man receives a wealth that grows day by day
And glory and also the powers that adorn the hero's way.|3|

When Agni pervades throughout the sacrifice's consummation
Verily to the Gods, reaches the performer's aspiration.|4|

The sacrificial overlord, the seer, the doer, the truth of ascension
The God brings the other Gods too to our dimension.|5|

With Thy purifying touch of Grace, you make all auspicious
O Angiras! This is your truth, most conspicuous.|6|

O Agni, Dispeller of flaws, we come closer to you each day
Bringing with us our thoughts of consecration, to you we pray.|7|

O custodian of Truth, Over all the sacrifices, king like you preside
May you flourish and progress in the home you reside.|8|

May we reach you, as a son does a father with ease
O Agni, May your benefaction upon us never cease!|9|

Know your Rishi: **Madhuchhandas Vaishwamitra**

The legendary sage, known for his mastery over the Vedas was also known for his melodious singing and the distinct rhythm and flow that he imparted to the Vedic hymns; his very name was a combination of two words Madhu- nectar and Chhandas – rhythm. The first 10 hymns of the First Mandala of the Rig Veda were composed by him. He was the son of the Legendary Vedic Rishi Vishwamitra and a brother of Sushruta –the Ayurvedic Physician who is recognized as the father of modern plastic surgery and the Vedic Rishi- Shunahshepah (the adopted son of Vishwamitra).

3 AGNI AND THE LEGEND OF THE ANGIRAS

Even a cursory glance at the Rig Veda reveals the symbolism that exists embedded within it. In the first hymn, we saw how Rishi Madhuchhandas chanted his honey-rhythm in an ode to Agni and paid homage to the mystic fire, proclaiming Him to be the herald of the Gods. According to him, Agni was not just the nature element of fire glorified as a deity. He was a living and conscious power that purified the mortal soul and instilled and furthered the inner aspiration in mortals, emancipating man and actuating his evolution towards Godhood. For Madhuchhandas, the Divine Agni was approachable by all; one could reach Agni in a manner similar to that of a son righteously approaching his father and his approach was rather direct and straightforward. However, this one line in the hymn- *'O Angiras! This is your truth, most conspicuous'* did leave some loose ends prompting a number of questions

"Who is Angiras?", "What is this truth of Angiras?", "Is Angiras and Agni one and the same?" We also come across the plural Divine entities together called Angirases, who are treated like the founding sages, the sons of Agni, the discoverers of fire and sometimes exalted to the status of Gods viz. the companions of Indra; at times Brihaspati himself is addressed as Angirasa.

"In the Brahmanas, it is said that Agni is the fire and the Angirases are the burning coals, angaaraah; but in the Veda itself the indication seems rather to be that they are the flames or lustres of Agni" - Sri Aurobindo, CWSA Vol 10, p. 156.

These allegorical references make it all the more fascinating and also empirical for us to understand the truth of Angiras. However, one thing is certain -both Agni and the Angirases are inexplicably linked.

We shall be attempting to explore and relate to this link to better understand the legend of Angiras and in the process also re-connect with, and relate to the mystic spirit of Agni- the God and Priest of the Vedic sacrifice. We look here at another Hymn to Agni composed by the Rishi Bharadwaja – Hymn 11 of the sixth Mandala.

यजस्व होतरिषितो यजीयानग्ने बाधो मरुतां न प्रयुक्ति ।
आ नो मित्रावरुणा नासत्या द्यावा होत्राय पृथिवी ववृत्याः ॥ ६.०११.०१
त्वं होता मन्द्रतमो नो अध्रुगन्तर्देवो विदथा मर्त्येषु ।
पावकया जुह्वा३ वह्निरासाग्ने यजस्व तन्वं१ तव स्वाम् ॥ ६.०११.०२
धन्या चिद्धि त्वे धिषणा वष्टि प्र देवाञ्जन्म गृणते यजध्यै ।
वेपिष्ठो अङ्गिरसां यद्ध विप्रो मधु च्छन्दो भनति रेभ इष्टौ ॥ ६.०११.०३
अदिद्युतत्स्वपाको विभावाग्ने यजस्व रोदसी उरूची ।
आयुं न यं नमसा रातहव्या अञ्जन्ति सुप्रयसं पञ्च जनाः ॥ ६.०११.०४
वृञ्जे ह यन्नमसा बर्हिरग्नावयामि स्रुग्घृतवती सुवृक्तिः ।
अम्यक्षि सद्म सदने पृथिव्या अश्रायि यज्ञः सूर्ये न चक्षुः ॥ ६.०११.०५
दशस्या नः पुर्वणीक होतर्देवेभिरग्ने अग्निभिरिधानः ।
रायः सूनो सहसो वावसाना अति स्रसेम वृजनं नांहः ॥ ६.०११.०६

O *Agni*, priest of sacrifice –O powerful and fiery force
Aid us in this mortal journey - bar the forces that oppose.
Towards *Mitra* and *Varuna*, May our offerings be consecrated

And the twin lords of heaven & earth, may our paths be directed | 1|

You bring us no harm, amongst us you are our God of invocation
O Priest Divine, in you we realize unparalleled bliss and perfection
Consume into your blazing mouth with the fiery tongue that purifies
Accept your own body as the worship and offering of sacrifice|2|

In You, a rapture and Godly understanding is housed
And in man the wisdom of the divine births and descents is aroused
When the wisest of the *Angiras* seers sings the revealed word
And in the sacrifice, his sacred honey-rhythm is heard |3|

Into the refulgence and light, O Agni - he does verily wade
Summiting the earth and heaven, may your sacrifice pervade.
All the five peoples bow in a puissant and complete submission
To the all granting and living fire, they offer their finest oblation |4|

When to Agni, the plucked sacred grass is offered in prostration
When the ladle's offerings to Agni are poured in consecration
Upon the earth, the abode of Agni is then truly ordained
And like an eye in the sun, the sacrifice is ingrained |5|

Empower us, O Son of Force, O priest of sacrifice
O consort of Gods, lend us the treasures of your paradise,
With your flaming armies of light on our side, may we assail
Overcoming the battle, beyond sin may we verily sail |6|

In this Hymn, we see that the Rishi Bharadwaja has taken a more cryptic approach embellishing his hymn with a rich imagery which often leaves space for multiple interpretations. For instance a literal interpretation of *Panchajanah*, or the five peoples in Verse 4, as the western Indologists very much prefer, implies that the sage was referring to the members of five specific Vedic tribes - Anus, Druhyus, Yadus, Turvasas, and Purus that find mention in the Rig Veda. A symbolic interpretation of the same vers implies that all the five types of people involved in the sacrifice bow in complete submission. The five types include the Yajamana (the host on whose behest the sacrifice is done) and the four Ritwiks Hotar, Udgata, Adhvaryu and Brahma.

The wisest Angiras could represent the wisest among the Ritwiks, present and performing the chants in the perfect manner or even the Yajamana. However, in the light of the first hymn of the Veda where the sage proclaims that the truth of Angiras is most conspicuous, this lets us understand that the truth of Agni cannot be only a perfect mortal chanting the hymns or an individual sage. Sri Aurobindo has already approached this problem and highlighted the solution for us. He has clearly pointed out that the Angirases are not just the human sacrificers but are the extension of the Divine Agni, the divine children of the mystic flame, the rays that very much possess the same powers and properties as their flaming source. It is this approach that is most pertinent for us in our quest.

"..Agni in the Veda is the light of the sun and the lightning as well as the flame found in the waters and shining on the earth. The Angiras Rishis being powers of Agni share this manifold function" – Sri Aurobindo, CWSA, Vol 10, p. 164.

The first two verses of the 31st Hymn of the Ist Mandala of the Rig Veda begin with the words *"Tvam Agne* 'O Agni, you are the very first Angiraah/Angirah' very clearly revealing the truth of the Angiras legend. It becomes obvious to us that Angiras and Agni are not just inexplicably linked but rather Agni is himself the first Angrias.

"Thou, O Agni, wast the first Angiras, the seer and auspicious friend, a god, of the gods; in the law of thy working the Maruts with their shining spears were born, seers who do the work by the knowledge" – Sri Aurobindo, CWSA, Vol 10, p. 165.

Understanding this truth of Angiras and their dual powers of knowledge and action is essential for it helps us in understanding the Agni-Agniras link, the Indra-Angiras link, Brihaspati-Angiras and also the connection of the Angiras with the Divine dawn, Usha. This is one very fascinating aspect of the Veda where we find a unique differentiation, integration and also transformation of the various God powers which are very interchangeable in their functions. It is only in this light that we can understand the true meaning of the appeal of the Rishis to the various god powers to become Angiras. This prayer to the Godheads to attain Angriashood is seen in the hymns directed towards both the Male Gods: Indra (Mandala 1, Hymn 100) and the Female Gods: Usha (Mandala 7, Hymn 79). The interchangeability of the God powers is manifest in most hymns and the symbolic approach allows us to conclude that the legendary Angirases are divine when they are associated or become one with the god powers and mortal when they function in the realized and awakened Vedic rishis.

With this conclusion we have not only succeeded in being introduced to the legend of the blazing Angiras but have also readied a ground on which we may touch another symbolism that is often repeated throughout the Vedic hymns – that of the holy cow and the kine of Veda.

Know your Rishi: **Bharadwaja Brihaspatya**

Rishi Bharadwaja is one of the most revered Vedic sages and is one of the seven venerated sages who are cited more than three times throughout the Rig Veda. He has authored several treatises on Medicine, Spirituality, Phonetics and even Archery. The Bharadwaja gotra was named after him and even today, his descendants continue to bear his name to further their proud association with his unbroken lineage. The classical Ayurvedic text, Charaka Samhita, mentions Rishi Bharadwaja and states that the Vedic sage performed penance to Indra seeking his blessings to improve the health of the people so that all are disease-free to progress in their life's spiritual journeys. In the Buddhist text, Digha Nikaya, the Buddha is quoted naming Bharadwaja as one among the ten noted Vedic sages.

4 THE COW, THE BULL & THE LUMINOUS HERDS

Another motif that is recurrent in the Vedic hymns dedicated to almost all the major deities is the image of the cow. The theme of the cow, the stolen cattle and the great victory that is celebrated upon retrieval of the cattle is neither tautological nor vestigial in purpose. Rather, it has a definite significance and origin. While the cow has always been revered in India since ancient times and is considered a source of prosperity even today, it would be quite banal to assume that the sages were so distracted by the prosperity that was to be obtained from the physical cows that they devoted so many verses to kine in the Veda. In some verses, the esoteric significance is so prominent and obvious that one cannot even logically assume that 'cows' refers to the physical herds. The second hymn to Agni in the fifth Mandala composed by Rihsi Vrisha Jana is one such hymn which directly displays the symbolic and esoteric purpose of the cattle found in the Vedas and so we will now explore that hymn.

कुमारं माता युवतिः समुब्धं गुहा बिभर्ति न ददाति पित्रे ।
अनीकमस्य न मिनज्जनासः पुरः पश्यन्ति निहितमरतौ ॥ ५.००२.०१
कमेतं त्वं युवते कुमारं पेषी बिभर्षि महिषी जजान ।
पूर्वीर्हि गर्भः शरदो ववर्धापश्यं जातं यदसूत माता ॥ ५.००२.०२
हिरण्यदन्तं शुचिवर्णमारात्क्षेत्रादपश्यमायुधा मिमानम् ।
ददानो अस्मा अमृतं विपृक्वत्किं मामनिन्द्राः कृणवन्ननुक्थाः ॥ ५.००२.०३
क्षेत्रादपश्यं सनुतश्चरन्तं सुमद्यूथं न पुरु शोभमानम् ।
न ता अगृभ्रन्नजनिष्ट हि षः पलिक्नीरिद्युवतयो भवन्ति ॥ ५.००२.०४
के मे मर्यकं वि यवन्त गोभिर्न येषां गोपा अरणश्चिदास ।
य ईं जगृभुरव ते सृजन्त्वाजाति पश्व उप नश्चिकित्वान् ॥ ५.००२.०५
वसां राजानं वसतिं जनानामरातयो नि दधुर्मर्त्येषु ।
ब्रह्माण्यत्रेरव तं सृजन्तु निन्दितारो निन्द्यासो भवन्तु ॥ ५.००२.०६
शुनश्चिच्छेपं निदितं सहस्राद्यूपादमुञ्चो अशमिष्ट हि षः ।

एवास्मदग्ने वि मुमुग्धि पाशान्होतश्चिकित्व इह तू निषद्य ॥ ५.००२.०७
हृणीयमानो अप हि मदैयेः प्र मे देवानां व्रतपा उवाच ।
इन्द्रो विद्वाँ अनु हि त्वा चचक्ष तेनाहमग्ने अनुशिष्ट आगाम् ॥ ५.००२.०८
वि ज्योतिषा बृहता भात्यग्निराविर्विश्वानि कृणुते महित्वा ।
प्रादेवीर्मायाः सहते दुरेवाः शिशीते शृङ्गे रक्षसे विनिक्षे ॥ ५.००२.०९
उत स्वानासो दिवि षन्त्वग्नेस्तिग्मायुधा रक्षसे हन्तवा उ ।
मदे चिदस्य प्र रुजन्ति भामा न वरन्ते परिबाधो अदेवीः ॥ ५.००२.१०
एतं ते स्तोमं तुविजात विप्रो रथं न धीरः स्वपा अतक्षम् ।
यदीदग्ने प्रति त्वं देव हर्याः स्वर्वतीरप एना जयेम ॥ ५.००२.११
तुविग्रीवो वृषभो वावृधानोऽशत्र्व१र्यः समजाति वेदः ।
इतीममग्निममृता अवोचन्बर्हिष्मते मनवे शर्म यंसद्धविष्मते मनवे शर्म यंसत् ॥
५.००२.१२

The youthful mother keeps the boy in concealment
Hidden even from the father, safe in her den,
His undiluted force though, escapes not the eyes of men
Who recognize his progression and inner movement|1|

"Who is this child that was carried by you?
O Mother you had borne him after you grew.
Within your womb, several years went past
I saw him when he was born to you at last.|2|

From a distance, I saw his one tusk-golden
The luminous form, wielding many a fearsome weapon
When my immortal ambrosia, to you I offer completely
Can the Indra-less and wordless ever harm me? |3|

In the field, I witnessed the herd luminous and beautiful
He was born now and they were safe and blissful
None could dare seize them in his reign
Even the greying old turned young once again|4|

Who weakened me, severing me from my herds of light?
Before, I had no defender or hero-warrior to fight!
I order the forces, "Release my light back to me."
Now aware, he drives them back, I can clearly see.|5|

The forces hostile hide the King who in all resides
The mortals dwell in him, not knowing that he presides
May they be liberated by Atri's words of wisdom
May the ensnarers themselves ensnared become|6|

With a thousand bonds, to the sacrifice Shunahshepa was bound
But You set him free and his liberation was found
O Priest, the rightful place within us, May you take
Conscious Lord, Set us free, let all our shackles break.|7|

May your wrath upon me, never be
Desert me not, For your secret was revealed to me
By Indra-Guardian of the laws of Gods, who sought
And realized your way and then to me he taught!|8|

This fire- Agni pervades all with its glory blazing
And by his might alone, all existences come to being
Conquering the forces nefarious in working and way,
Whetting his horns, the evil Rakshasa he seeks to slay.|9|

May his fiery roar as a weapon function
And bring about the Rakshasa's destruction
The hostile forces seek to contain and capture
But fail for he rages on untouched in his rapture|10|

O One of births many, this hymn, May you envisage
A vehicle offered by the best worker, thinker and sage
Accept my offering, so we may win the light-stream
O Lord, and the celestial waters too of the sun-realm|11|

The strong necked bull juggernauts across hostile forces
Developing, Driving away from opposers knowledge's sources
Thus the immortals spoke of the fire's divine functioning
Bringing peace to man as he readied the seat, offering. |12|

While we can see that this hymn is decorated with a number of riddles which warrant an in-depth understanding of the lexical verb-plays and symbolisms adopted by the composer, some verses explicitly convey to us that the cow, the herds and the bull do not in any way refer to the actual physical creatures. They have a distinct and significant spiritual reference. For instance, with reference to Verse 4, Sri Aurobindo had raised the following questions that clearly undermined a purely physical interpretation of the hymns.

"What, we may fairly ask, are these shining herds, these cows who were old and become young again? Certainly, they are not physical herds,

nor is it any earthly field by the Yamuna or the Jhelum that is the scene of this splendid vision of the golden-tusked warrior god and the herds of the shining cattle" - Sri Aurobindo, CWSA Vol 15, p. 142.

The Sukta opens with the rich symbolism of a mother concealing a child from the father after bearing it in her womb for several years. Obviously, this child is no mortal child and the mother no human mother. Sri Aurobindo points out to us that the child is Agni himself and the mother is the mother Earth.

"Agni, long repressed in her womb by mother Earth who is unwilling to give him to the father Heaven, held and concealed in her so long as she is compressed into limited form (peshi), at length comes to birth when she becomes great and vast (mahishi). The birth of Agni is associated with the manifestation or vision of luminous herds." – Sri Aurobindo, CWSA Vol 15, p. 141.

If we study the verse in this light, the luminous herds become the symbols of the Divine illumination. When Agni was born and realized (within), the herds were safe and joyous for now Agni would ensure that the Divine illumination received would not be harmed or stolen by the forces of darkness.

"They are radiances that were stolen by the powers of darkness and are now divinely recovered not by the god of the physical fire, but by the flaming Force which was concealed in the littleness of the material existence and is now liberated into the clarities of an illumined mental action" – Sri Aurobindo, CWSA Vol 15, p. 142.

Before the clarity of the illumined mind was realized, the chanter was confounded by the action of the hostile forces which weakened him by taking away his strength- his herds of light. The frustration is palpable in the words 'Before, I had no defender or hero-warrior to fight'. But with the blessing of the illumined mind, by the grace of Agni, everything changed. Summoning the strength of the new found Agni in him, Vrisha Jana orders the forces of darkness to return the clarities that were unjustly taken away from him, preventing him from gaining the full realization of the truth. Now that Agni had arisen, the forces that bind would themselves be bound. The wisdom of Atri's words would drive away the ignorance that prevented man from realizing the Divine who resideds in all. Recollecting the tale of Rishi Shunahshepa he prays that his bonds too be removed in the same way. According to the legend, the young Shunahshepa was tied to the sacrificial post to be offered as sacrifice but the hundred bonds that tied him disappeared as he invoked Usha (The Divine Dawn) while he was chanting his Vedic hymns. Recognizing Agni's grace in this feat, Vrisha Jana proclaimed that he had been granted the realisation of the secret of Agni by the guardian of the Gods- Indra, who had himself realized the way to Agni. In his hymns he says that Agni was the cause of the manifestation of all living things, destroyer of the forces of darkness. He envisions Agni as a blazing bull sharpening his horns to gore the forces of evil and bring about the destruction of the Rakshasa. The forces, with nefarious plans, surround the Divine bull seeking to contain him but the juggernaut force razes the forces that seek to conceal the wisdom. The sage, perfect in action, highest in thought, invites the dynamic Divine force to be seated in the vehicle that he has fashioned with his hymns so that they may together win the light streams and the waters of the celestial world of the sun.

While the riddles of the celestial waters and the light steams of the Sun still remain to be solved, we can satisfactorily state with confidence that we now know the significance of the cow, the bull and the luminous herds mentioned in the Rig Veda. This readies the ground on which we may seek to understand the truth of the 'Mother of the cows' of the Veda, whose path even the Sun follows – Mother Usha.

Know your Rishis: **Kumara Aatreya**

Vrisha in Sanskrit means 'Bull' literally. This makes the name of the composer of this hymn – Vrisha Jana all the more apt and exact. Another name for Vrisha Jana is Kumara Aatreya, who belongs to the lineage of the Atris. It may be noted that Vishnu too is referred to as a bull in the Veda. We will be elaborating on this during a separate introduction to Vishnu later on.

Atri is the last of the seven celestial sages revered as the Saptarishis. The fifth Mandala of the Rig Ved, also known as the Atri Mandala, contains 87 hymns composed by Atri and his successors, together called the Atreyas or the Atris. These hymns are known for their distinct style of concealment of spiritual ideals in the form of riddles. Atri is one of the most frequently mentioned sages in the Rig Veda and is also mentioned in the Ramayana as residing in the Chitrakuta Forest Ashram.

His wife is Anusuya who, according to the legend, was known to be one of the legendary seven Pativratas. Her piety and devotion enabled her to attain great powers which made it possible for her to produce three sons –Dattatreya, Durvasa and Soma, all of them immaculate conceptions and avatars of the divine Trinity: Brahma, Vishnu and Maheshwara.

5 USHA – THE DAWN DIVINE

Usha the Goddess is both the Mother of all the Gods and also the Divine dawn of the luminous truth and not merely a personified deity of Day and the mother of the cows as propounded by the naturalistic interpretation of the Veda. While we do come across repeated references to Usha as the mother of the Cows in different verses of the Veda, Sri Aurobindo points out to us that the cow in the Veda is but a symbol of the light of spiritual illumination. The Gods are the bestowers of the light of spiritual truth in man and by this ratiocination, we can very well state that the Divine mother of the cows is also the mother of the Gods.

"Usha as the mother of the cows can only be a form or power of this supreme Light, of this supreme Consciousness, of Aditi. And in fact, we do find her so described in I.113.19. maata devaanaam aditer aneekam, " Mother of the gods, form (or, power) of Aditi" – Sri Aurobindo, CWSA Vol 15, p. 131.

Once this understanding of Usha as a form of Aditi is established, we can proceed to explore the real meaning of the Dawn of the Veda. Also, by this analogy we can further state that her counterpart, Night, or Ratri, is but a form of Diti, the counterpart of Aditi and the mother of the *Danavas*, or the non-divine forces that prevent the manifestation of the Divine light in man and hinder his progress.

We thus see that the Rishis of the Vedas with divine mastery concealed the esoteric sense by applying the symbolism of night and day to the darkness of ignorance and the dawn of truth respectively, so that only the initiated would be able to understand that Usha is but a form of the Divine Mother, by whose grace the inner darkness is dispelled completely and the Dawns of new consciousness are born in man.

With this approach, we too can become aware and understand what lies behind the symbolisms of the "New Dawns" and "New Births" that are oft repeated in the Vedic hymns. The path of dawn is not just the path of the physical Sun but rather the way of the supreme truth or Ritam.

"We have precisely the same idea repeated but with still clearer and fuller psychological indications in I.124.3; ritasya panthaam anveti sadhu, pajaanateva na disho minaati: "She moves according to the path of the Truth and, as one that knows, she limits not the regions."

Another psychological function of Usha can be established in the verse *I.113.16*

उदीर्ध्वं जीवो असुर्न आगादप प्रागात्तम आ ज्योतिरेति ।
आरैक्पन्थां यातवे सूर्यायागन्म यत्र प्रतिरन्त आयुः ॥ १.११३.१६

Awaken, O soul, for the Life has returned
The light approaches and darkness has been overturned
She has paved the path for the sun to travel
And we have arrived where life can limitlessly unravel|16|

Here we can clearly observe that Mother Usha, the paver of the path of the sun, plays a crucial role in reviving the life and awakening the soul. She casts her light and raises man to a place where the full potential of life can unravel unhindered by any of the opposing forces. However, even if we were to cast aside the psychological aspects of the divine Dawn and observe the purely physical phenomenon of dawn, we would be able to observe and perceive- the rhythm divine that plays in the early hours of each day, also known in many Indian regional languages as the *"Ushah Kaal"or* the "Time of Usha". Every morning, all the living components of nature get revived and awakened from a dark night's slumber. Probably it was because the dawn of a new day was something so innately spiritual, that the Rishis of the Vedic Era chose to cloak the truth of Goddess Usha in the symbolism of the physical dawn.

Some more fascinating aspects of the psychological functions of the divine Dawn can be found in the 61st Hymn of the third Mandala composed by Vishwamitra, Gathinah.

We shall now look at the rhyme rendition of the same in light of Sri Aurobindo's luminous commentary and translation of this Hymn.

उषो वाजेन वाजिनि प्रचेताः स्तोमं जुषस्व गृणतो मघोनि ।
पुराणी देवि युवतिः पुरंधिरनु व्रतं चरसि विश्ववारे ॥ ३.०६१.०१
उषो देव्यमर्त्या वि भाहि चन्द्ररथा सूनृता ईरयन्ती ।
आ त्वा वहन्तु सुयमासो अश्वा हिरण्यवर्णां पृथुपाजसो ये ॥ ३.०६१.०२
उषः प्रतीची भुवनानि विश्वोर्ध्वा तिष्ठस्यमृतस्य केतुः ।
समानमर्थं चरणीयमाना चक्रमिव नव्यस्या ववृत्स्व ॥ ३.०६१.०३
अव स्यूमेव चिन्वती मघोन्युषा याति स्वसरस्य पत्नी ।
स्व१र्जनन्ती सुभगा सुदंसा आन्ताद्दिवः पप्रथ आ पृथिव्याः ॥ ३.०६१.०४
अच्छा वो देवीमुषसं विभातीं प्र वो भरध्वं नमसा सुवृक्तिम् ।
ऊर्ध्वं मधुधा दिवि पाजो अश्रेत्प्र रोचना रुरुचे रण्वसंदृक् ॥ ३.०६१.०५
ऋतावरी दिवो अर्कैरबोध्या रेवती रोदसी चित्रमस्थात् ।
आयतीमग्न उषसं विभातीं वाममेषि द्रविणं भिक्षमाणः ॥ ३.०६१.०६
ऋतस्य बुध्न उषसामिषण्यन्वृषा मही रोदसी आ विवेश ।
मही मित्रस्य वरुणस्य माया चन्द्रेव भानुं वि दधे पुरुत्रा ॥ ३.०६१.०७

O Opulent Dawn, endowed with wisdom and strengths great
O Dawn, accept these chants, by which we venerate-
The Goddess both ancient and youthful, swift in motion
Bestower of boons and for the actions, granter of sanction.|1|

Immortal Goddess Dawn, May your moon-chariot blissfully shine
To reveal the soothing voice of the Truth Divine
The lustrous golden horses radiate your ever flowing refulgence
Leading you to us so we may realize your magnificence|2|

Accosting and raising the worlds in their every multitude
With your immortal understanding, standing at the highest altitude
Traversing the plains with equal measures, proceeding on your way
Wheel like O Dawn, you summon the morn of the new day.|3|

The consort of bliss moves endowed with abundant richness
Letting her robe fall, she spreads Svar's blissfulness
With perfection in action and enjoyment she spreads
When from the heavens onto the earth she treads.|4|

Surrender to her and she shines on to you
Channel all your energies as she comes to your view
To the heaven's zeniths is her force's ascension
Its sweetness and bliss, she brings into our mortal dimension.|5|

In her we can receive the heaven's ruminations
Our mind and body firmaments, by her attain truth's illuminations
To that Dawn, seeking her bliss's essence Agni prays
And attains the complete delight by her light rays|6|

Into the vast worldly firmaments, the Lord forays
Embedding truth's constitution into the Dawn's rays
Varuna's wisdom and Mitra's harmony, He together blends
The light of happy oneness to all forms, He lends.|7|

We see Goddess Usha venerated by the sage in the very first verse of the hymn wherein he declares that she is the opulent and wise granter of all boons. Though ancient, she is ever youthful and swift in her movement and all mortal actions occur by her sanction alone. Usha is envisioned in her brilliant moon-chariot yoked to wide and vast golden horses that lead her from her celestial abode to the earthly plane. Her psychological function is perfectly highlighted in the next verse where the sage proclaims that the Goddess of the Divine Dawn uplifts the world by first accosting its limitations and then raising it by lending her immortal perspective from her high abode in the celestial heavens. She turns the wheel of darkness and brings in man the birth of a new dawn. Spreading the bliss of *Svar* into the world by her swift motion she lets her robe fall from the heavens to blanket the earth and instil perfection in both action and enjoyment.

The Rishi calls upon man to surrender all of his capacities and energies to the Divine Mother Dawn and bask in her light as she approaches closer to man, for she verily brings with her the sweetness and the happiness of the highest heavens where she dwells. Her illumination is the illumination of the truth consciousness in man; Agni too fervently seeks the Light rays of Usha to attain his fulfilment.

The Supreme Lord of all beings enters into the world by establishing His truth in the light rays. Through the foundation of the Dawn, the Divine establishes the foundations of His truth by blending together the wisdom of Varuna and the harmony of Mitra.

"Dawn divine is the coming of the Godhead. She is the light of the Truth and the Felicity pouring on us from the lord of Wisdom and Bliss, amritasya ketuh, svarasya patni." - Sri Aurobindo, CWSA Vol 15, p. 298.

With this understanding of the real significance of Goddess Usha, we are now ready to approach and understand the functions of Varuna- the feared oceanic deity who is also known to ruthlessly punish sinners in order to uphold the Divine law.

Know your Rishis: **Vishwamitra Gathinah**

Rishi Vishwamitra is one of the most respected of Vedic Rishis and is credited with the authorship of most of the suktas of the Third Mandala of the Rig Veda. He finds mention in both the Ramayana and Mahabharata and in various Puranic tales. He is recognized as the preceptor of Rama and the knowledge of the divine weapons or Devaastras was imparted to Rama by him. He was believed to have been an efficient king before he left his kingdom to do penance and become widely accepted as a BrahmaRishi. His real name was Kauhika but he was later known as Vishwamitra, 'Friend of the World', due to his universal compassion for all being. He is the father of Madhuchhandas, Sushruta, Shunahshepa and Shakuntala.

6 THE TRUTH OF VARUNA

In most places in the Rig Veda, Varuna appears in conjunction with Mitra, but as our objective is to be introduced to the Devas of the Vedas one after another, we will be examining Varuna independently.

Not too long ago, Varuna the titan God was equated with Uranus, the Greek God of the sky and this interpretation was accepted by the most erudite scholars but now this comparison has been rendered untenable and dubbed a philological error. 'The God of the Sky', 'The Vanquisher of foes', 'The Upholder of the Laws', are some of the personalities that have been assigned to the Godhead due to different interpretations of various Vedic verses. But holding any one of these interpretations as absolute and ignoring the others has only led to a repetition of the same errors. The problem arises because of the flawed logic of the naturalistic and ritualistic theory of the Veda which attempts to confine within rational limits, in this case, an all pervading God whose ever increasing vastness only spreads in all directions.

Sri Aurobondo's Integral Psychological Theory of Interpretations offers the best solution. According to Sri Aurobindo, Varuna is the *'all-pervading Vastness and purity of the Divine supporting and perfecting the world'*. He is the granter and upholder of the Law of truth, and terrible destroyer of all the foes and forces that prevent the growth and progression of a man on the path of truth. He is the highest heaven and also the lowest abyss, the compassionate God who bestows grace and also the terrible Titan who destroys with rage.

"Varuna in the Veda is always characterised as a power of wideness and purity; when, therefore, he is present in man as a conscious force of the Truth, all that limits and hurts the nature by introducing into it fault, sin and evil is destroyed by contact with him. He is ri's ¯adas, destroyer of the enemy, of all that seek to injure the growth"- Sri Aurobindo, CWSA, Vol 15, p. 76.

It is in this spirit, that we shall approach Varuna. I have chosen the 25th Sukta of the first Mandala written by the Rishi Shunashepah because it is one of the few hymns were Varuna has been singly invoked and also because it is, incidentally, the very first Hymn of the Rig Veda that I learnt by heart after being instructed by my teacher, Damleji.

यच्चि॒द्धि ते॒ विशो॑ यथा॒ प्र दे॑व वरुण व्र॒तम् ।
मि॒नी॒मसि॒ द्यवि॑द्यवि ॥ १.०२५.०१
मा नो॑ व॒धाय॑ ह॒त्नवे॑ जिहीळा॒नस्य॑ रीरधः ।
मा हृ॑णा॒नस्य॑ म॒न्यवे॑ ॥ १.०२५.०२
वि मृ॑ळी॒काय॑ ते॒ मनो॑ र॒थीरश्वं॒ न संदि॑तम् ।
गी॒र्भिर्व॑रुण सीमहि ॥ १.०२५.०३
परा॒ हि मे॒ विम॑न्यवः॒ पत॑न्ति॒ वस्य॑इष्टये ।
वयो॒ न व॑स॒तीरुप॑ ॥ १.०२५.०४
क॒दा क्ष॑त्र॒श्रियं॒ न॒रमा वरु॑णं करामहे ।
मृ॒ळी॒कायो॑रु॒चक्ष॑सम् ॥ १.०२५.०५

तदित्समानमाशाते वेनन्ता न प्र युच्छतः ।
धृतव्रताय दाशुषे ॥ १.०२५.०६
वेदा यो वीनां पदमन्तरिक्षेण पतताम् ।
वेद नावः समुद्रियः ॥ १.०२५.०७
वेद मासो धृतव्रतो द्वादश प्रजावतः ।
वेदा य उपजायते ॥ १.०२५.०८
वेद वातस्य वर्तनिमुरोर्ऋष्वस्य बृहतः ।
वेदा ये अध्यासते ॥ १.०२५.०९
नि षसाद धृतव्रतो वरुणः पस्त्या३स्वा ।
साम्राज्याय सुक्रतुः ॥ १.०२५.१०
अतो विश्वान्यद्भुता चिकित्वाँ अभि पश्यति ।
कृतानि या च कर्त्वा ॥ १.०२५.११
स नो विश्वाहा सुक्रतुरादित्यः सुपथा करत् ।
प्र ण आयूंषि तारिषत् ॥ १.०२५.१२
बिभ्रद्द्रापिं हिरण्ययं वरुणो वस्त निर्णिजम् ।
परि स्पशो नि षेदिरे ॥ १.०२५.१३
न यं दिप्सन्ति दिप्सवो न द्रुह्वाणो जनानाम् ।
न देवमभिमातयः ॥ १.०२५.१४
उत यो मानुषेष्वा यशश्चक्रे असाम्या ।
अस्माकमुदरेष्वा ॥ १.०२५.१५
परा मे यन्ति धीतयो गावो न गव्यूतीरनु ।
इच्छन्तीरुरुचक्षसम् ॥ १.०२५.१६
सं नु वोचावहै पुनर्यतो मे मध्वाभृतम् ।
होतेव क्षदसे प्रियम् ॥ १.०२५.१७
दर्शं नु विश्वदर्शतं दर्शं रथमधि क्षमि ।
एता जुषत मे गिरः ॥ १.०२५.१८
इमं मे वरुण श्रुधी हवमद्या च मृळय ।
त्वामवस्युरा चके ॥ १.०२५.१९
त्वं विश्वस्य मेधिर दिवश्च ग्मश्च राजसि ।
स यामनि प्रति श्रुधि ॥ १.०२५.२०
उदुत्तमं मुमुग्धि नो वि पाशं मध्यमं चृत ।
अवाधमानि जीवसे ॥ १.०२५.२१

O Overlord Varuna, the laws of truth that we must comply
We the mortals, day by day only verily defy.|1|

Yield us not to the attacks of death, be appeased
May your destructive rage on us, never be released.|2|

Like the horse reins that a charioteer uses to yoke
Binding your heart, your forgiveness, these hymns seek to invoke.|3|

Moving away from me, the material desirers simply take flight
Like the birds of the sky, returning to their nests to alight.|4|

When shall you reveal to man, the 'Hero Warrior of might'?
O Varuna, Bless the mortals with your Grace and foresight!|5|

For this, they all verily and joyously accept
And unfailingly offer prayers in your respect.|6|

O Knower of the celestial pathways and the birds of the heavens,
And also the routes of the seas and vessels of the oceans|7|

O Knower of all the births that the 12 moons bear
And also the manifestations that are yet to appear|8|

O Knower of the great wind-paths spreading high and wide
You even know all the Gods that in the upper realms reside.|9|

Varuna- the conscious one upholding his pledge, verily presides
Governing all with wisdom, along with the mortals he resides.|10|

From here He oversees the wondrous rapture of the creation
And the acts completed and those that are to come to fruition.|11|

Making the world receive Aditya-the sun's illumined days
For every soul, you prolong their earthly stays.|12|

Draped in a mantle of gold, radiating light you are seated found
O Varuna, your spies too are present around.|13|

One who is hurt not by enemies nor those who harm the clan
You are the God who destroys the enemies of man.|14|

Favoring man, with unparalleled glory you bless
Uplifting us too, you grant (integral) physical progress|15|

Like cattle thirsting for the meadows, my eyes aspire
To see the clairvoyant Lord mighty, I verily desire.|16|

May our dialogue that once was, once more resume
This sweet nectar, your offering favorite, may you consume.|17|

The hymns have been accepted, a vision has been granted to me
I saw his celestial carriage hovering above, now the world too can see.|18|

O Varuna, hearken to my desperate cries
May your benevolence pour from your mighty skies|19|

To you, O wise Overlord of the world, I pray
Heed my call today, before journeying ahead on your way.|20|

Untie the bonds above, loosen the middle ones, may the one's below dissolve
From all the shackles, release me so my life can truly evolve.|21|

Thanks to Shunahshepah and his hymn, we too are able to perceive a vision of Varuna as his celestial car hovers above mortals. Varuna, the king is seated on his throne not in his heavenly abode but in the kingdom of mankind along with his subjects. Surrounded by his spies, draped in a mantle of gold, he is conscious of the occurrences of things at all times and places. Feared and respected, the overlord watches over his subjects on earth, sea and sky to ensure that they journey on truth's path, destroying all that harms growth and progress. He is the upholder of truth-consciousness in the universe and he is the breaker of all the bonds that chain man and keep him away from the the path of truth preventing the soul's progress.

With this, we are now ready to move from the vast oceanic overlord to the one who consumes the Soma and perfects the forms with his illuminations, Indra, the lord of the Devas

Know Your Rishi: **Shunahshepa Aajigarti**

Rishi Shunahshepa was the middle and least wanted son of Sage Ajigarta. According to the tale of the Aiteriya Brahmana, he was offered by his father, who readily gave him up, in exchange for hundreds of cattle, to be the sacrificial object for the Rajasuya yagnya of King Harishchandra. Tied to the sacrificial post, he began reciting his hymns to Varuna and invoked all the deities in proper succession. following the instructions he received intuitively; ultimately he earned his liberation and the Gods untied and blessed him. Sage Vishwamitra then adopted him as his spiritual son and named him Devarata – the one obtained from the God.

7 INDRA – THE LORD OF THE ILLUMINED MIND

Indra in the Puranic stories has been reduced to a personified Lord of Devas and bringer of rain, residing in the Heavens as a Divine king leading all the Gods in Zeusian fashion in their battles against the demons/asuras. In the Jataka tales, we find Indra to be a hero-god displaying several human traits and flaws, such as anger, arrogance, and lust which, more often than not, land him in several unwanted situations leading to his becoming subject to the samsaric cycles of birth and death. While the lore of Indra and his inconic image with a thunderbolt weapon-Vajra and his white elephant-Airavat has survived over generations, Indra's Vedic significance and origin has been blurred and completely effaced from the minds of the masses. This makes it all the more necessary to understand the truth of Indra in the spirit of the Rig Veda.

Sri Aurobindo, in his secret of the Veda, has described the psychological functions of *Indra* to be associated with mind-power stating that the very name indra is derived from the sense faculties *indriya*. If we observe the general order of deities invoked by the different seers in the various Mandalas of the Veda, we find that Indra is invoked immediately after the hymns in invocation of Agni after which the other deities are invoked. When looking at Indra's role in the Veda in the Sri Aurobindonian way, we find the recurring theme of Indra slaying the concealers of light, the Vritras, the Valas, the python and other subconscient powers, while the thunderbolts and flashing lightnings reveal to man the illuminations that were hidden from him.

Sri Aurobindo calls Indra the lord of the illumined mind and as it is our objective to understand Indra's role in shaping the mental formations in man, we will take a look at the 170th verse of the 1st Mandala which portrays a dialogue between the sage Agastya and Indra himself, perfectly elucidated by Sri Aurobindo in "The Colloquy of Indra and Agastya"

न नूनमस्ति नो श्वः कस्तद्वेद यदद्भुतम् ।
अन्यस्य चित्तमभि संचरेण्यमुताधीतं वि नश्यति ॥ १.१७०.०१
किं न इन्द्र जिघांससि भ्रातरो मरुतस्तव ।
तेभिः कल्पस्व साधुया मा नः समरणे वधीः ॥ १.१७०.०२
किं नो भ्रातरगस्त्य सखा सन्नति मन्यसे ।
विद्मा हि ते यथा मनोऽस्मभ्यमिन्न दित्ससि ॥ १.१७०.०३
अरं कृण्वन्तु वेदिं समग्निमिन्धतां पुरः ।
तत्रामृतस्य चेतनं यज्ञं ते तनवावहै ॥ १.१७०.०४
त्वमीशिषे वसुपते वसूनां त्वं मित्राणां मित्रपते धेष्ठः ।
इन्द्र त्वं मरुद्भिः सं वदस्वाध प्राशान ऋतुथा हवींषि ॥ १.१७०.०५

Indra said:
That which is at this moment, absent
That which tomorrow too is not present
Who is it that has been able to grasp or capture?
Who has understood its wondrous rapture?
It acts and flows in another's consciousness
It disappears, when sought through one's mental prowess.|1|

Agastya asked:
O Indra, Why must we face the wrath of your might?
The Maruts, are but thy brethren of the divine light
Through them, the desired perfection may your reach
But slay not our spirit's attempt and outreach |2|

Indra asked,
Why, O brother Agastya, Are you not my friend?
Beyond me, why does your thought seek to portend?

I know very well what you have sought,
Without seeking to lend to us your mind and thought!|3|

With the understanding the altar you can construct
Let Agni blaze in the front, you may thus instruct
For there the consciousness will immortal awake
When in the sacrifice, you and I shall together partake| 4 |

Agastya agreed:

You are the lord supreme, ruler of all the living
Overlord of friendships, you reign as the king

O Indra, with the mighty Maruts may you agree
Accept and enjoy the offerings, as per the solemn decree.|5|

In just five verses, this sukta is completed but the significance of the verses and the cryptic inferences display to us the functions of Indra with perfect clarity. We understand that Indra is the master of all the living in the realm of the living, *vasunam vasupate*, loving friend and lord of friendships, *mitranam mitrapate* who actively participates when mortals perform the sacrifice.

He is aware of the thoughts that form in the mind, vidma he te yatha mano and his presence is most necessary for the mortal soul's outreach to the higher domains of the spirit. He is the actuator of the inner journey and it is only when the force of aspiration of the soul is coupled with Indra's sanction that the harmonious completion of the sacrifice with the awakening of the immortal consciousness in man takes place.

Sri Aurobindo has perfectly described this union of Indra and Agastya as the joining of the universal power and the human soul.

"Let the egoistic endeavour cease, the great sacrifice be resumed, the flame of the divine Force, Agni, be kindled in front as head of the sacrifice and leader of the march. Indra and Agastya together, the universal Power and the human soul, will extend in harmony the effective inner action on the plane of the pure Intelligence so that it may enrich itself there and attain beyond. For it is precisely by the progressive surrender of the lower being to the divine activities that the limited and egoistic consciousness of the mortal awakens to the infinite and immortal state which is its goal." – Sri Aurobindo, CWSA Vol 15, p. 255.

Know Your Rishi: **Agastya Maitravaruni**

Rishi Agastya is one of the revered Saptarihsis and many hymns of the 1st Mandala are attributed to Agastya and his wife Lopamudara. However, his origins and lineage remain a mystery as it is believed that Rishi Agastya was a human descendent of the Gods Mitra and Varuna, hence the name Maitravaruni. He is prominently mentioned in the Ramayana, Mahabharata and Puranas, is considered to be the father of the Tamil language and is the compiler of the first work on grammar, Aggatiyam.

8 SOURA SUKTAM – A HYMN TO SURYA

Though modern science acknowledges the sun to be the source of life for all life forms on earth, the reason why the winds blow across the seasons, and the entity around which all the heavenly bodies revolve, it has a rather dry understanding of the sun as a blazing lifeless mass of a broken star which is burning itself towards its explosion. However as we can see, even the most scientific ratiocination cannot hide the poetic rapture that is concealed behind the veil. It was this beauty of the Sun that inspired the Mayans, the Aztecs, the Incas, the Celtic and even the ancient civilizations across the African, Chinese, Greek and Baltic regions who worshipped the Sun with devotion.

In India too, sun worship thrived and. even today, the sun has a great cultural significance. In most traditional households, the day begins with the physical activity called Surya Namaskara or sun salutation and the recitation of the 12 names of the Sun which describe the 12 different functions of the sun viz, Mitra- the friend of all, Ravi- the bringer of transformation, Surya- the one who induces activity, Bhanu- the one who gives all light, Khaga- the one who moves in the sky, Pusha – the one who nourishes all, Hiranyagarbha- the one with the golden womb that bears all, Maricha – the bringer of the dawn , Aditya- the first solar lord of gods, Savitra- the lord of the truth, Arka – the essence of all, Bhaskara – the shining and lustrous one.

While this practise is nowadays widely popularised as a healthy life style exercise and reverence for the Sun has survived the onslaught of time, there is a need to look at the Vedic origin of Surya.

The Vedic Civilizations not only recognized the divinity of the sun but also arrived at several scientifically significant truths with a great deal of accuracy without sacrificing the spiritual significance of the Sun. Most scientists are still finding it mind boggling to lean how the Vedic Indians arrived at accurate astronomical figures aeons before the first telescope was invented. This only sheds light on the fact that science and spirituality need not be antipodal and it is in this light that we shall seek to understand the Sun as perceived by the Vedic Seers.

"The Solar energy is the physical form of Surya, Lord of Light and Truth, it is through the Truth that we arrive at Immortality, final aim of the Vedic discipline. It therefore under the images of the Sun and its rays, of Dawn and day and night and the life of man between the two poles of light and darkness that the Aryan seers represent the progressive illumination of the human soul" – Sri Aurobindo, Vol 15, CWSA, p 289.

A sukta for Surya first appears in the 50th Hymn of the First Mandala of the Rig Veda composed by the famous Vedic Seer Praskanva Rishi. We will look at this here.

उदु त्यं जातवेदसं देवं वहन्ति केतवः ।
दृशे विश्वाय सूर्यम् ॥ १.०५०.०१
अप त्ये तायवो यथा नक्षत्रा यन्त्यक्तुभिः ।
सूराय विश्वचक्षसे ॥ १.०५०.०२
अदृश्रमस्य केतवो वि रश्मयो जनाँ अनु ।
भ्राजन्तो अग्नयो यथा ॥ १.०५०.०३
तरणिर्विश्वदर्शतो ज्योतिष्कृदसि सूर्य ।
विश्वमा भासि रोचनम् ॥ १.०५०.०४
प्रत्यङ्देवानां विशः प्रत्यङ्ङुदेषि मानुषान् ।
प्रत्यङ्विश्वं स्वर्दृशे ॥ १.०५०.०५
येना पावक चक्षसा भुरण्यन्तं जनाँ अनु ।

त्वं वरुण पश्यसि ॥ १.०५०.०६
वि द्यामेषि रजस्पृथ्वहा मिमानो अक्तुभिः ।
पश्यञ्जन्मानि सूर्य ॥ १.०५०.०७
सप्त त्वा हरितो रथे वहन्ति देव सूर्य ।
शोचिष्केशं विचक्षण ॥ १.०५०.०८
अयुक्त सप्त शुन्ध्युवः सूरो रथस्य नप्त्यः ।
ताभिर्याति स्वयुक्तिभिः ॥ १.०५०.०९
उद्वयं तमसस्परि ज्योतिष्पश्यन्त उत्तरम् ।
देवं देवत्रा सूर्यमगन्म ज्योतिरुत्तमम् ॥ १.०५०.१०
उद्यन्नद्य मित्रमह आरोहन्नुत्तरां दिवम् ।
हृद्रोगं मम सूर्य हरिमाणं च नाशय ॥ १.०५०.११
शुकेषु मे हरिमाणं रोपणाकासु दध्मसि ।
अथो हारिद्रवेषु मे हरिमाणं नि दध्मसि ॥ १.०५०.१२
उदगादयमादित्यो विश्वेन सहसा सह ।
द्विषन्तं मह्यं रन्धयन्मो अहं द्विषते रधम् ॥ १.०५०.१३

He is the God who knows everything
Who bears, with his rays every living thing
Appearing in the world's line of sight|1|

Even the constellations take flight
From thy illumining self, like thieves sly
For the whole world you behold in your eye|2|

The peoples of the distant world perceive
Through the rays, the God they verily see
Blazing like the flames of the fire|3|

O Surya, your light, you cause all to acquire
You direct the world to become resplendent,
And the world too reflects your light refulgent|4|

You rise in the realms of the Godly clan
And also in the mortal world of man
The rise of the sun the universe does truly witness |5|

With the same grace you verily bless
And nourish the living for their progress,
Varuna's progression too you watch and assess.|6|

Greeting all with your light beams
Wading through the skies and the heavenly realms
O Surya, The births of all beings you witness|7|

The chariot of seven steeds, O God Surya you harness,
With your luminance, all things you illuminate
And your effulgent hair too does verily radiate|8|

Yoking the seven chariot bearers pure
The onward progression of your car you ensure
Thus together you further proceed|9|

Shining your light upwards, darkness you supersede,
Among the Gods, the most divine and prominent
And among lights, we seek Surya, the most brilliant|10|

Rise today, O great friend and ascender
Luminous Lord, to the light realms yonder
O Surya, Rid the disease of my heart
May the paleness in me verily depart.|11|

May the weakness within leave and perish
The parrots and the saplings may it nourish
Feeding on it may the green plants grow
May my feebleness thus completely go.|12|

With the dawn of Aditya, we see the skies
In the world, his victory and rise
May my enemies, I verily overcome
Their prey, May I never become|13|

Thus, if we perceive the sun in this light, we understand that Surya is the nourisher who removes all forms of darkness and weaknesses in man and the one who ensures the ripening of the consciousness in man to enable the divine realization.

if we absorb the energy of the sun by basking in His rays of truth, no other energy will be necessary in our lives to further our growth because the Surya is himself Narayana – a form of Vishnu who nourishes the lives of all micro and macroscopic forms of plant and animal lives and is also the cause of the various natural phenomenon in our universe.

Krishna in the Gita while describing the various Vibhutis or cosmic representations of the Divine to Arjuna states in the 21st Shloka of the 10th Adhyaya.

"Aadityanaam aham vishur jyotishaam ravir amshumaan",

Amongst Adityas, the seven suns, I am Vishnu the most radiant
Amongst splendorous lights, I am the brilliant sun.

With this preliminary introduction to the solar diety – Surya, we are now ready to move on to the next Vedic deity, the governor of all the movements of forces, winds and life, Vayu.

Know Your Rishi: **Praskanva Kaanvah**

Rishi Praskanva is the son of the Vedic Rishi Kanva, who adopted Shakuntala, the daughter of Rishi Vishwamitra in his Kanvaashram or hermitage. Seven suktas in the First Mandala, one in the Eighth and another in the Ninth Mandala are attributed to the Rishi Praskanva.

9 THE FLOW OF VAYU

Vayu had a greater significance as the true overlord of all the life energies in Vedic age than his outer meaning might suggest; we are now familiar with this outer meaning as a result of the personification of the deity over several generations from the post Vedic Era onwards. We understand that Vayu was personified as the God of the wind in the epics Ramayana, where he was the father of the Rudra, Hanuman or in the Mahabharata where he fathered the mighty Pandavan prince Bhima, and also in the Puranic lores where Vayu's wrath led to the cessation of the movement of all winds and air putting the very existence of all creatures at risk. However, the true origins of Vayu have a deeper and more profound meaning. The Rishis of the Veda perceived the psychological functions of Vayu in attaining the highest realizations and found, concealed within the symbols embedded in their sweetly sung hymns, great truths expressed with an unparalleled subtleness and ingenuity in such a way that only the initiated would grasp the higher purpose of the hymns. Vayu, as the master of the life energies has control over the domain of every life. The Prana, or life force entering and leaving the living, the flow of the winds across the world and all types of movements can be attributed to Vayu. The Vedic seers recognized this and also the other psychological functions of Vayu in the completion and manifestation of the incomplete and unmanifest. Among the various Vedic Rishis, Sri Aurobindo offers his greatest praises to Rishi Vamadeva for his hymnal creations invoking Vayu in different ways and singles out the 48th hymn of the fouth Mandala of the Rik Veda in his commentary on Vayu in his "Secret of the Veda" as one of his finest works.

Though this sukta contains only 5 shlokas, it displays the cryptographic prowess of the Vedic Rishis in concealing the esoteric meanings through outward symbols. If not for Sri Aurobindo's key and elucidation, the true meaning of the verses might have never reached us.

Let us look at the sukta a little more closely

विहि होत्रा अवीता विपो न रायो अर्यः ।
वायवा चन्द्रेण रथेन याहि सुतस्य पीतये ॥ ४.०४८.०१
निर्युवाणो अशस्तीर्नियुत्वाँ इन्द्रसारथिः ।
वायवा चन्द्रेण रथेन याहि सुतस्य पीतये ॥ ४.०४८.०२
अनु कृष्णे वसुधिती येमाते विश्वपेशसा ।
वायवा चन्द्रेण रथेन याहि सुतस्य पीतये ॥ ४.०४८.०३
वहन्तु त्वा मनोयुजो युक्तासो नवतिर्नव ।
वायवा चन्द्रेण रथेन याहि सुतस्य पीतये ॥ ४.०४८.०४
वायो शतं हरीणां युवस्व पोष्याणाम् ।
उत वा ते सहस्रिणो रथ आ यातु पाजसा ॥ ४.०४८.०५

That which never manifested may you manifest
As the priests offer you sacrificial works, best
Come, O Vayu, in your refulgent car divine
Partake in the savouring of the Soma wine.|1|

Yoke your steeds, dispel the obstructions
With Indra as charioteer, let flow your expressions
Come, O Vayu, in your refulgent car divine
Partake in the savouring of the Soma wine.|2|

The two dark (realms) perceive you in their actions
Enclosed within them are all manifestations
Come, O Vayu, in your refulgent car divine
Partake in the savouring of the Soma wine.|3|

May you be led by ninety and nine horses
Whom the mind yokes and harnesses
Come, O Vayu, in your refulgent car divine
Partake in the savouring of the Soma wine.|4|

With a hundred brilliant steeds controlled
O Vayu, may they increase many fold
Else may the horde of a thousand drive
Enabling your massive force to verily arrive|5|

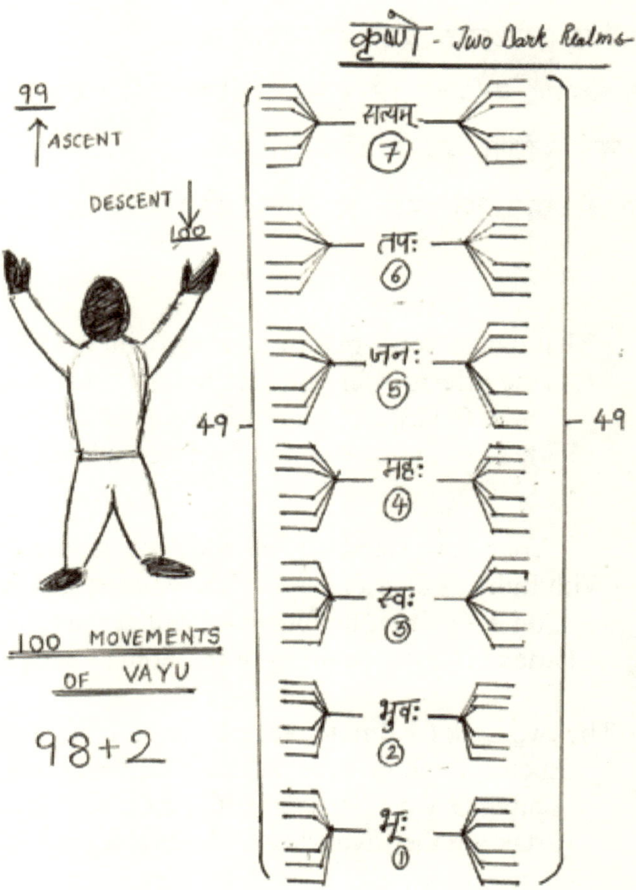

We see in the first four verses a repetition of the second line of the shloka wherein lies the request of Vamadeva inviting Vayu to arrive in his chariot that shines and radiates a light divine and accept the Soma offering. 'Soma' and 'ghrita' as Sri Aurobindo points out are not just the offerings of wine or clarified butter respectively. While the clarified butter represents the clarified mental consciousness, the soma drink refers to the Ananda or pure bliss which is the true immortal elixir that can descend upon the mortal from the realm of the immortal.

"*The "secret Name" of the mental consciousness, the tongue with which the gods taste the world, the nexus of Immortality, is the Ananda which the Soma symbolises*" - Sri Aurobindo, CWSA Vol 15, p. 307.

Vayu verily brings about the manifestation of the unmanifest and his movement removes the obstacles and lets flow the expression of the divine. The chariot of the master of life is yoked to the steeds that shine and radiate a blissful light and his charioteer is none but Indra - the master of the mind.

While these symbolisms are easy enough to understand, the references to the 'Two Dark' *Krishne* and the specific implication of the numbers ninety-nine, a hundred and a thousand in the succeeding verses does pose some questions regarding the purpose behind these seemingly arbitrary references.

The hymns were certainly not the compositions of irrational or confused minds and, as we have seen, in hymns before that, each time a reference is truly discovered, a hidden world of great vastness and spiritual meaning is opened for us to behold. It is in Sri Aurobindo's light that the veil is lifted and we are able to truly grasp at least a glimpse of the wonder that was experienced by Vamadeva when he made this composition.

The 'Two Dark' or two black unnamed existences refer to the black side of the earth and the heaven, the physical and the mental consciousness that craves to be illuminated.

"It is their dark states- the obscured consciousness between its two limits of the mental and the physical,- which by the happy movement of the nervous dynamism begin to labour in accordance with the movement or under the control of Vayu and to yield up their hidden forms; for all forms are concealed in them and they must be compelled to reveal them" - Sri Aurobindo, CWSA Vol 15, p. 312.

Likewise a coherent meaning of the increasing number of horses or the energies that are to be manifested from 99, 100 and finally to1000 also becomes clear to us in light of Sri Aurobindo's elucidation for, with an ace mathematician's precision, he identifies an arithmetical progression that can lead us to the numbers using the principles of addition and multiplication.

He postulates that we begin with the mystic figure 7, which represents the seven forms of divine consciousness that manifest in nature. (eg. The seven existences Bhur, Bhuah,Swaha, Maha, Janah, Tapah & Satyam).

Each existence contains another six within itself. Thus we have a total of 7 × 7 existences equalling 49. As there are two, a duplication of all of them takes place, one for the upward movement and another for the downward descent of the energies. We arrive at the number 98 (49 × 2); one more unit which corresponds to the ascent of man to the luminous plane and another unit corresponding to the final descent of the Gods into the obscure plane of man takes us to the figure of a 100.

Now, when we see the verses 4 & 5 in this light, it all begins to make sense.

The ninety-eight horses when yoked to the mind become the ninety and nine horses which are one step away from completion, for here the upward ascent is complete. In the next verse the completion is visible through the number 100 where the descent of Vayu and Indra is described and Vama deva recognizes the power of Vayu and the potential of the forces to increase in sync with the general vedic theme of the ever expanding truth, *satyam rtam brihat.*

In his final hymn to Vayu, Vamadeva offers a choice for the descent to take place. He requests Vayu to arrive with his hundred steeds, complete in all respects to be nourished and increase after arrival, or else he calls upon Vayu to arrive unbridled in a gush with his massive force of a thousand steeds (100 X10). This aspiration of Vamadeva is articulated perfectly by Sri Aurobindo,

"It is the completely varied all-ensphering, all-energising mental illumination with its full perfection of being, power, bliss, knowledge, mentality, vital force, physical activity that he desires." - Sri Aurobindo, CWSA Vol, 15, p. 314.

This sukta, though among the shortest I have come across, is definitely one of the deepest. I believe we too can invoke Vayu in our lives once we establish the necessary conditions in our mental, physical, vital and psychic beings and stand upon the same pedestal of Vamadeva with arms open wide asking Vayu to choose to descend with his hundred steeds that will multiply and spread horizontally, or to descend in a massive flow with his thousand steeds at once. The grace is there as it has always been, but if the vessel to receive it on the ground is not ready, no descent can ever take place.

With this introduction to Vayu, we are now ready to connect to Vishnu.

Know Your Rishi: **Vamadeva Gotama**

Rishi Vamadeva son of the Rishi Gautama is credited with many suktas of the Fourth mandala. He was the son of the Maharishi Gautamam, one of the Saptarishis and brother of Nodhas Rishi who also authored various suktas. The hymns of Mahadeva are distinct in style and find their mention in the Aiteriya and Brihadarnyaka Upanishads which contain the foundations of the Vedantic school of thought.

10. VISHNU – THE FRIEND OF MAN

Vishnu in India is revered as the manifesting preserver among the Trinity of the Divine Supreme, the one who descends to mankind's aid to restore the balance of the world and to ensure the continuation and progress of all worldly existences. His incarnations are called Avatars and every Hindu scripture recognizes 10 Avatars of Vishnu called the Dashavatars, nine of which have already manifested in different epochs of time.

From the *Matsya* (Fish- Aquatic), *Kurma* (Tortoise- Amphibious), *Varaha* (Boar – Terrestrial) in the animal kingdom, *Narasimha* (Man-Lion) a transitional consciousness and then the human Avataars, *Vamana* (Dwarf man), *Parashu Rama* (the mighty ax wielding one), *Rama* (The One with the perfectly Divine mental consciousness), *Krishna* (The One with the Overmental consciousness) and *Buddha* (The One who merged into the supreme nil). *Kalki*, the final Avatar, who is yet to manifest is believed to be the One who will complete the task that has remained unfinished by the previous nine Avatars. An evolutionary sequence is observed in the Avatars; Sri Aurobindo calls the ten Avatars a parable of evolution.

While the scriptural and structurally organized significance of Vishnu is fascinating, it makes one all the more curious to understand the significance of Vishnu as attributed by the Vedic Rishis. Let us look at the 154th Hymn of the Mandala I which is dedicated to Vishnu by the Rishi Dirghatamas

विष्णो॒र्नु कं॑ वी॒र्या॑णि॒ प्र वो॑चं॒ यः पार्थि॑वानि विम॒मे रजां॑सि ।
यो अस्क॑भाय॒दुत्त॑रं स॒धस्थं॑ विचक्रमा॒णस्त्रे॒धोरु॑गा॒यः ॥ १.१५४.०१

प्र तद्विष्णु॑ः स्तवते वी॒र्ये॑ण मृ॒गो न भी॒मः कु॑च॒रो गि॑रि॒ष्ठाः ।
यस्यो॒रुषु॑ त्रि॒षु वि॒क्रम॑णेष्वधिक्षि॒यन्ति॒ भुव॑नानि॒ विश्वा॑ ॥ १.१५४.०२
प्र विष्ण॑वे शू॒षमे॑तु॒ मन्म॑ गिरि॒क्षित॑ उरुगा॒याय॒ वृष्णे॑ ।
य इ॒दं दी॒र्घं प्रय॑तं स॒धस्थ॒मेको॑ विम॒मे त्रि॒भिरित्प॒देभि॑ः ॥ १.१५४.०३
यस्य॒ त्री पू॒र्णा मधु॑ना प॒दान्यक्षी॑यमाणा स्व॒धया॒ मद॑न्ति ।
य उ॑ त्रि॒धातु॑ पृथि॒वीमु॒त द्यामेको॑ दा॒धार॒ भुव॑नानि॒ विश्वा॑ ॥ १.१५४.०४
तद॑स्य प्रि॒यम॒भि पाथो॑ अश्यां॒ नरो॒ यत्र॑ देव॒यवो॒ मद॑न्ति ।
उ॒रु॒क्र॒मस्य॒ स हि बन्धु॑रि॒त्था विष्णो॑ः प॒दे प॑र॒मे मध्व॒ उत्स॑ः ॥ १.१५४.०५
ता वां॒ वास्तू॑न्युश्मसि॒ गम॑ध्यै॒ यत्र॒ गावो॒ भूरि॑शृङ्गा अ॒यासः॑ ।
अत्राह॒ तदु॑रुगा॒यस्य॒ वृष्णः॑ प॒र॒मं प॒दमव॑ भाति॒ भूरि॑ ॥ १.१५४.०६

Of his deeds mighty, I thus proclaim
Measurer of earthly realms- Vishnu, I verily name
Striding wide with only footsteps three
From the zenith, so we can all realized be |1|

Atop his abode, up the high mountains treacherous
With mighty deeds, striding like a lion ferocious
All the worlds, within his three movements wide
And all the living things, find a place to reside.|2|

May we channel our force and our thinking
Towards Vishnu- the wide moving taurine being
Who wearily measured from the mountain residence
In whose three steps is our place of existence. |3|

In His three steps is contained the nectar sweet
Imperishable, the experience is with ecstasy replete
All the worlds, the heavens and the earth he holds
By the triple principle, all the living he verily beholds|4|

The happy realms that the god-seekers aspire to gain
And his rapture too, May I experience and verily attain
It is here that the highest friend of man resides
Sweetness' source is Vishnu of the mighty strides |5|

In your abodes, we seek our journey's realization
For the nimble light herds, it is the destination
The many horned ones in your vast realms roam
As you shine down light from your home |6|

In Dirghatamas's hymn we see a very different form of Vishnu from the various familiar forms that we see in the Vaishnava tradition. He is described as a fierce lion roaming in his lair atop the mountains and also like a mighty bull who strides across the earth. His deeds are valorous and mighty and Dirghatamas declares to us that the greatest deed done by Vishnu was measuring existence.

He states that Vishnu measured the earth and the other realms of existence with his three wide steps and within this space all living creatures dwell. The taurine mentioned in this sukta is definitely no ordinary being but is a clear symbol of Vishnu as a cosmic bull that wades in the realms that are up from and beyond the earthly existence.

It is interesting to note that the mystical three steps of Vishnu seem like precursors to the fifth Avataar of Vishnu, *Vamana* (the Dwarf man). Vamana was also known as *Trivikrama* meaning the victor over the three worlds: the heavens, the earths and the nether realms. However, the three strides of the Vedic Hymn differ greatly from the three steps taken by the *Vamana* Avataar to send the titan *Bali* to the nether planes.

"*The three strides of Vishnu in the Veda are clearly defined by Dirghatamas as earth, heaven and the triple principle, tridhaatu. It is this triple principle beyond heaven or superimposed upon it as its highest level, naakasya prishte, which is the supreme stride or supreme seat of the all-pervading deity.* ". - Sri Aurobindo, CWSA Vol 15, p. 336.

Further, we find Dirghatamas mentioning the abode of Vishnu as a realm of happiness that is imperishable, symbolizing the bliss of the immortal divine realization. He calls Vishnu, the highest friend of man and states that it is his realm that all the god seekers aspire to attain as the destination, and that the realization is but a rapturous experience of undiluted bliss. The many horned herds of light roaming in his abode do not refer to actual kine grazing but rather are symbols of illumination and realization much like the symbol of the Vedic Cow. With this introduction we are ready to understand the significance of Goddess Saraswati.

Know Your Rishi: **Dirghatamas Auchithya**

Rishi Dirghatamas was the son of Utathya Rishi and has Twenty-five suktas in the First Mandala; he is the leading Rishi of the Goutama clan and is the brother of Rishi Bharadwaja. The rishis Gautama, Nodhas and Vamadeva were his successors. Dirghatamas, literally meaning "long darkness" was the name given to him as he was born blind. Among his suktas, the one which contains the line "ekam sat viprah bahudha vadanti" is most notabe because it speaks about the overall oneness of the gods, directly disproving the western vedic theory which stated that the verses of the Vedas were purely pantheistic in nature.

11. SARASWATI- THE RIVER AND THE GODDESS

If there is any description of a Vedic deity where the symbolism is crystal clear and impossible to mask, it is in the hymns to the female goddess Saraswati. The stream Saraswati is also the deity and this is by no means a mere naturalistic personification of the river Sarasawti. Specific psychological functions and an awakened consciousness has been recognized and associated with her. The Vedic Rishis considered that the divine Saraswati is different from all the streams and is associated with creation, intuition and inspiration.

This facet of Saraswati has survived over the ages and today the Vedic Goddess Saraswati is worshipped in different forms across India, Myanmar, Japan, Cambodia and even Thailand. In the Mahabharata, she is called the Veda Mata or the Mother of the Vedas and in the Puranas she is said to have assumed different forms to assist in new creations across the earth and is considered to be the goddess of wisdom and a counterpart of the goddess of wealth, Lakshmi. A wonderful Sanskrit stotra on Saraswati calls mother Saraswati "*Vedayai, Vedarupayai, Vedantayai*" the one who is Veda, the form incarnate of Veda and the culmination of the Veda, Vedanta. Though there is a stark difference between the Saraswati of the Veda and the image of goddess Saraswati, the functionality and significance is not too diferent.

Let us now look at the 95th hymn of the VII mandala where Vasishtha has invoked the goddess Saraswati.

प्र क्षोदसा धायसा सस्र एषा सरस्वती धरुणमायसी पूः ।
प्रबाबधाना रथ्येव याति विश्वा अपो महिना सिन्धुरन्याः ॥ ७.०९५.०१
एकाचेतत्सरस्वती नदीनां शुचिर्यती गिरिभ्य आ समुद्रात् ।
रायश्चेतन्ती भुवनस्य भूरेर्घृतं पयो दुदुहे नाहुषाय ॥ ७.०९५.०२
स वावृधे नर्यो योषणासु वृषा शिशुर्वृषभो यज्ञियासु ।
स वाजिनं मघवद्भ्यो दधाति वि सातये तन्वं मामृजीत ॥ ७.०९५.०३
उत स्या नः सरस्वती जुषाणोप श्रवत्सुभगा यज्णे अस्मिन् ।
मितज्ञुभिर्नमस्यैरियाना राया युजा चिदुत्तरा सखिभ्यः ॥ ७.०९५.०४
इमा जुह्वाना युष्मदा नमोभिः प्रति स्तोमं सरस्वति जुषस्व ।
तव शर्मन्प्रियतमे दधाना उप स्थेयाम शरणं न वृक्षम् ॥ ७.०९५.०५
अयमु ते सरस्वति वसिष्ठो द्वारावृतस्य सुभगे व्यावः ।
वर्ध शुभ्रे स्तुवते रासि वाजान्यूयं पात स्वस्तिभिः सदा नः ॥ ७.०९५.०६

Saraswati, Streaming in a gush, strong as a metal fort
Offers with her waters, nourishment and support
On a chariot, onwards the oceanic one goes
Surpassing all the the streams, she verily flows |1|

Among the rivers, from the mountains to the ocean
Saraswati alone flows conscious in her motion
Providing her milk and richness aplenty
To all the ones living in her vicinity |2|

The male power grew amidst the feminine presence
From the sacrifice grew a child of fertile essence,
To the accomplished ones, He offers his mettle
And cleanses his body for the victory in battle |3|

May Saraswati be delighted and pay heed
As we approach her in sacrifice and plead

With bent knees, our reverence when we offer
Her kinship is granted for her comrades to prosper |4|

Offered in your obeisance may you verily accept
This hymn, O Saraswati, chanted in your respect
Place us in your refuge, become our protector
As under a tree, may we be in your shelter |5|

Vasishtha opened, O Divine Saraswati be pleased
Doors that were closed, so you may be appeased
In the singer, shine brighter and further grow
With your blessings, to highest states may we go|6|

In this hymn Vasishta invoked the Goddess Saraswati, all powerful in her flow which was very different from all the other streams. Mighty as a metallic fort, the goddess ensured the sustenance of the peoples. What markedly separated Sarasawati from the other streams was her movement. While the other streams merely flowed from the mountains to the oceans, Sarasawati was the true stream of inspiration, awakened in her conscious flow granting all the dwellers in her vicinity an awakened consciousness which grows enriched by the fertility of the feminine presence, purifying the body and imparting strength to ensure a true victory.

Obeisance is paid to the all-powerful goddess by shedding one's ego, symbolized by the bending of the knees in surrender to her sovereignship. And when this act is performed, the worshipper is recognized as a comrade of the Goddess and prosperity is but a consequence of her kinship. Like refugees seeking the shelter of a tree, chanters of the hymns to Saraswati seek to be under her aegis and invoke her with respect. Vashishta proclaims his great victory by declaring that the doors that were closed for Saraswati were opened by him and so he invites the Goddess to grow in the chanter and grant her blessings and illuminations so that the seeker may go to the highest stages.

The symbolic and esoteric meaning of the Vedic hymn to Saraswati is thus unmistakable and clearly established. We are now ready to move to the last hymn of the Rig Veda. It will be interesting to see which deity or power is invoked in the final hymn.

Know Your Rishi: **Vasishtha Maitravaruni**

Rishi Vasishtha is amongst the most revered sages and is considered to be one of the legendary seven sages. He is chief author of the suktas of the 7th Mandala and the hymns of most of this Mandala bear the stamp of the Vasishtha family. Credited with the authorship of multiple Puranas and Vedic Suktas, he is best known for the scripture "Yog Vasishtha" and the Vedantic Sermon that he offered to Rama. Among his many disciples Bhisma is a prominent character of the Mahabharata.

12. THE HYMN TO MAN- THE LAST SUKTA

Before we proceed to the final hymn of the Rig Veda, let us re-examine the conclusions that we have drawn.

We saw how the Agni of the Angiras sages is not just the personification of the physical fire but the deeper flame of aspiration rising within man to create an atmosphere conducive to the manifestation of the divine. We also recognized that the cows, bulls and horses are not the physical creatures that ensure material wealth but rather the shining and luminous herds that symbolize the illuminations from the divine planes that were observed in the ruminations of the vedic rishis. Usha is not a personification of the physical dawn bur rather the dawn of a new consciousness on the plane of man. Varuna, the omnipresent king and upholder of law, ensures the reign of truth consciousness and removes all the useless bonds that chain the individual, preventing him from realizing his true and fully divine potential. Indra the lord of the gods is but the lord of the illumined mind, accelerating the journey towards completion and perfection in life. Surya, is not just the visible physical sun but also the divine sun that ensures a widening of consciousness by removing of all that is dark, weak and unripe in man.

The roaring winds of Vayu are not just the physical winds or gods who grant horses to the singers of the hymns. Rather, Vayu facilitates the movements of ascension and descent that are necessary for the upward and downward spiritual movements that aid in the realization of the divine consciousness in man. The Vedic Vishnu is not the deity living in a mansion with cattle grazing around. He actuates the progress of the soul and is the destination of bliss that can be reached when realization is attained in man. And finally, Saraswati is not simply a river that the sages found to be nourishing and useful for feeding their people and livestock. She is the goddess that manifests as inspiration in man, banishing the weakness of the mind, granting the boons of new creations and existences when pleased, by dispelling one's individual egos.

With this in mind, we are now ready to look at the last hymn of the Rig Veda, which is the culmination of this great spiritual and ancient scripture. The first hymn is an invocation to Agni and the next three hymns are dedicated to Samgyanam – the knowledge of oneness among all beings. Let us have a look at the last sukta of the Rig Veda

संसमिद्युवसे वृषन्नग्ने विश्वान्यर्य आ ।
इळस्पदे समिध्यसे स नो वसून्या भर ॥ १०.१९१.०१
सं गच्छध्वं सं वदध्वं सं वो मनांसि जानताम् ।
देवा भागं यथा पूर्वे संजानाना उपासते ॥ १०.१९१.०२
समानो मन्त्रः समितिः समानी समानं मनः सह चित्तमेषाम् ।
समानं मन्त्रमभि मन्त्रये वः समानेन वो हविषा जुहोमि ॥ १०.१९१.०३
समानी व आकूतिः समाना हृदयानि वः ।
समानमस्तु वो मनो यथा वः सुसहासति ॥ १०.१९१.०४

We invoke Agni, mighty 'Lord of Fire', to come-
May the flames of the spirit kindled become.
For Thy comrade- The God within every being,
Shower His grace upon all-the living and non-living
United we – the world peoples stand and pour the libations
May the earth be nourished by our sacrificial oblations |1|

Together, may we progress, prosper and grow
The same knowledge, may we all know
May the language that we speak be one
United may all the minds assemble under the Sun.
May all the Gods their due shares-receive,
Satisfied, Their blessings-May the mortals achieve.|2|

May all offerings, chants and minds echo a sameness
May all of us become One in consciousness.
Becoming one in mantras and mind
All of us chanting and offering, may you find
May the sounds Divine chanted together resonate
The spirit of Oneness may we all impersonate.|3|

From an inner intuition may all utterances start
May the same oneness originate from every heart.
Make us together in our complete union
May all beings agree and live in a joyous communion.|4|

These verses by the seers that were chanted several thousand years ago make one's eyes well with tears. Ultimately the wise seers in their last verses turned to man with a selfless payer: may the race of man be united in spirit and consciousness and receive the blessings together and, finally, may all of mankind live in joyous communion.

Why is this prayer still such a distant dream? Will mankind ever awaken from the collective slumber to realize the awakened dream of the Rishis?

I am certain that the dream will not remain a dream forever and so I offer my prayers to the Devas and place my hopes in the alliance of man!

Know Your Rishi: **Sanvananah Aangirasah**

Rishi Sanvananah is of the lineage of the Angiras sages and the authorship of the last sukta is attributed to him. Other information about this Rishi is sparse but what is most notable about his final sukta is that after invoking Agni, he chooses to invoke the feeling of oneness among all beings for a peaceful and happy co-existence on earth. A perfect and fitting end to the colossal spiritual scripture.

EPILOGUE

In a hidden sanctum, veiled to mortal eyes -
Time readied to perform the yagnya of Fire on ice.
Barefooted -the banished one walked on frozen floor -
To appease Agni and take mankind's call to heaven's door.
With closed eyes, for the sake of man.
Escaping mortal lips- the sacred hymn began
"On the altar of truth, O Messenger of the Lords !
Heed my call as I invoke the Gods-|8|

Now has been lit the mighty fire sacred
May all that you devour turn consecrated.
O Agni! humble offerings I make at your sacred pyre
The sacrifice completed -may you accord what we aspire
These primal oblations now I pour into your fire
I offer my cherished dreams and all that I desire:
Like dead grass may these fuel you to greater grow -
Lift me higher with your flames - lend me your radiant glow!|16|

Now, I shed to you my flaws and all my vice:
Burn them to ashes, for with blood I have paid the price.
To serve you only, rid me of my imperfection and disease.
Come forth reside in me- from useless bonds offer me release.
Next into the fire I now joyfully pour -
Feasting on this may you fiercely roar.
My actions of past, present and the future time.
My Karma, My works and all that is mine.|32|

The final sacrifice this flawed mortal shalt now make -
Immaculate fire, my soul is now truly yours to take.
The same fire that now blazes before my eyes
Burns within me now, emancipating my rise.
The same fire that hath kindled the Sun -
See it burning, O Agni, in the eyes of the chosen one .
Consume this too, O, every God's harbinger
Time is ripe. Let darkness feel thy scorching anger.|40|

By your grace, I am now a part of you-
Now I can perceive the inferno that shalt ensue,
Holy one, Engulf this globe in your fiery cocoon
Help us establish a place for the gods to arrive soon.
Lord Agni! hither you have brought the Gods-
Once again these divine kings shalt reign over their wards.
Ashwini kumars of the nimble steed led by Indra-
Also have arrived mighty Maruts, Father Varuna and Mitra.|48|

Vayu, Surya, Vishnu and Rudra too have arrived
Vritras, Valas and Dasyus now have nowhere to hide
The bulls, the lion and the feral beasts of light-
Have all rushed in to join and banish the night.
Mother Usha walks towards us beckoning the dawn-
Saraswati, Ila and Sarama ensure that darkness has withdrawn!
O Vishwedewas come forth, ascend your golden throne,
And endow man with the ambrosia- Soma has sworn."|56|

The dream of the Rishis has true become
The time of cosmic Awakening has finally come
Earth now stands bathed in your supramental light
Redemption is now complete, darkness has taken flight.
She is now awake from her frozen slumber-
The golden destiny has been reached, now no force can encumber!|62|

Revelation of Truth: **The Aim of Midam Symbolized**

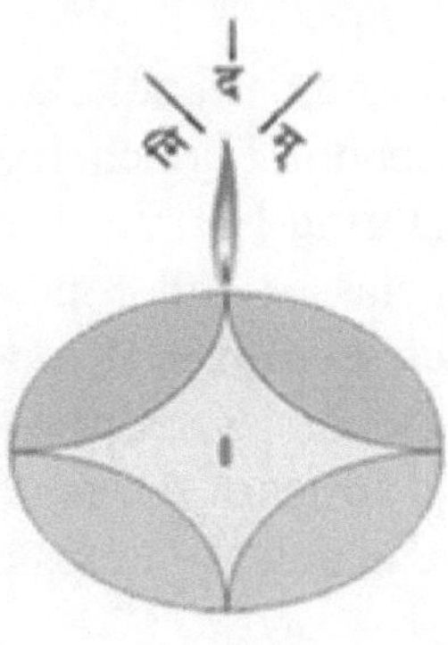

The meaning of the Midam Symbol envisioned by Damleji:-

The sphere represents the earth that we live on. The blue colour depicts the skies and green the flora and fauna. The yellow arched diamond represents man who is always in communion with the five elements.

Inside man is a tiny flame - the flame of aspiration which represents the *Chaitya Purusha* -"the psychic being". Man's aspiration takes him higher and higher to meet the supreme light represented by Agni.

This higher knowledge descends in man and he then embraces the earth having received this light- the knowledge, he uses it for the betterment of all life on earth.

Midam Charitable Trust's – The Krishna's Butter Project (For Kids & Adults)

In 2015 Krishna's Butter Project was started by Midam Charitable Trust, Pondicherry under the direction of its founder Sri Madhusudan Damle which led to the development of a Free teaching module and course book published by Midam titled, "Krishna's Butter For Champion Students" authored by senior Pathologist and ex.HOD, Dr.Bhawana Badhe and student of Sri Madhusudan Damle. This was later translated into Hindi and Marathi language by Sri Arvind Chandorkar, a retired banker and student of Damelji and the same was also published by the trust.

Dr.Bhawana Badhe took it to the school class rooms of the students of Class 8 of Vidhyaniketan School, Puducherry and this became a regular feature at their institute. During her free time especially in the weekend, she conducted more classes and connected with various parents and kids who enjoyed the classes. In 2018, one parent, Mrs.Chitra Torvi, a homemaker, was so happy after observing the positive changes in her 2 daughters that she began to learn the methodology of the Krishna's Butter Project and began teaching to interested persons.

In 2020, Once the lockdown started all schools were closed and Mrs. Chitra Torvi came up with the idea of taking it to the digital classrooms. And the module was adopted to suit the Digital platforms and online batches for children 8 and above were launched for children of all countries and backgrounds. **No fee is charged for these sessions** and all children are accommodated on First Come First Serve Basis. Avanti Badhe and Sushrut Badhe, both disciples of Sri Madhsudan Damle began conducting separate batches for kids and adults respectively after receiving the training to meet the demand for the classes.

So Far, 61 Batches have been launched including 15 batches for adults with over 3000 enrolments from participants in India, USA, UK, Canada, Australia, Singapore and Dubai.

KRISHNA'S BUTTER MODULE:

Taking the Practical principles of the Gita to children, a strong foundation of value education is laid on the basis on select 99 verses from Bhagavad Gita from all 18 chapters of the Gita over a period of 19 sessions on weekdays, with each session lasting for 45 minutes. Audio's of Sanskrit verses are provided and each day a cartoon illustration is shared matching the Lesson of the day and the shlokas are explained as English rhymes taken from "Bhagavad Gita : Rhythm of Krishna" written by Sushrut Badhe. Weekends are Off where participants share their questions which are answered by the Krishna's Butter core team. For the Adults, most of the verses of the Gita are covered with relevant day to day examples.

FEEDBACK RECEIVED:

We have received several feedbacks from parents that their kids have shown significant and positive behavioural changes. Improvements in creativity, reduction in shyness, improvement in confidence, anger control and overall happiness during the current period are a common theme in the feedback. Due to demand from happy parents asking for advanced courses, follow up batches called Krishna's Delight also have been started for a monthly meeting to revise on the practical principles of the Gita which children can practise in everyday lives.

The teachers were most impressed with children sharing their everyday experiences where they utilized the Concepts like Karma Yoga, doing things happily with detachment, asking for help from elders when in trouble like Arjuna and also how they grasped the nutritional concepts of food on the basis of Satvik- Rajasic –Tamasic Foods from the Gita.

Niharika Khanna, a participant from the Adults batch wrote to us "Insightful discussions, practical examples, new learnings that too, in the form of Rhythmic explanations, have strengthened the sense of our own duties, knowledge, ability, to discriminate between righteousness and wrong, value of dedication, true form of Dharma and list goes on and on". To know more about Midam, visit here: www.facebook.com/midamtrust or www.midamashram.org

Hi,

My sister, Avanti and I are working under our teacher- Sri Madhusudan R Damle at his unit, KVM Research Laboratories sharing the responsibilities as GM and CEO respectively. Together we manufacture and export 100% Natural Ayurvedic health and beauty products at our unit in Midam Ashram at Kothapurinatham Village.

To find out more about the KVM Project, visit here: www.ayurvedaforyou.in

To check out KVM's online store: www.amazon.in/herbomineral or scan this QR code on your smartphone.

- Sushrut Badhe

Other Midam Charitable Trust Publications:-

Bhagavad Gita simplified for kids:-

1. Krishna's Butter For Champion Students (English)
2. Krishna Navneet – Yashwant Chatron Ke Liye (Hindi)
3. Krishna Navneet – Yashwant Vidhyarthyansathi (Marathi)
4. Kannan te Naruvenna – Kuttikale samartharakkan (Malayalam)
5. Krishnarin Vennai – Sadanaipadaikkum manavarkalakku (Tamil)
6. Krishnana Navaneeta- Nyayakatva vidhyarthigalige (Kannada)

Entire Bhagavad Gita in poetic rhymes:

7. Bhagavad Gita Rhythm of Krishna

Coming Soon!

8. Nineteenth Adhyaya of the Gita & more…

ABOUT THE AUTHOR

The author is the disciple of Sri.M.R.Damle and is the CEO of KVM Research Laboratories, which was founded by Damleji in 1988. Located in Kothapurinatham village, Puducherry, the SSI manufactures and exports purely natural Ayurvedic products. He is, as well, a researcher at Midam Charitable Trust, also founded by his Damleji, which works in the fields of education, women empowerment and children with special needs and is actively engaged in the scientific investigation and evaluation of the therapeutic effect of listening to Vedic Chants.

The author holds a degree in mechanical engineering and has a liking for poetry. He has transcribed the entire Bhagavad Gita and some of the Upanishads: Isha, Kena, Mandukya and Sri Aurobindopanishad in rhyme and holds the records for the same in the India Book of Records and Limca book of records.

www.ingramcontent.com/pod-product-compliance
Lightning Source LLC
Chambersburg PA
CBHW050023170726
48282CB00025B/521
* 9 7 8 8 1 9 5 5 2 5 4 2 3 *